Un:Stuck

Un:Stuck

Helping Teens and Young Adults Flourish in an Age of Anxiety

KATE O'BRIEN

sheldon PRESS

First published by Sheldon Press in 2025

An imprint of John Murray Press

1

This book is for information or educational purposes only and is not intended to act as a substitute for medical advice or treatment. Any person with a condition requiring medical attention should consult a qualified medical practitioner or suitable therapist.

A CIP catalogue record for this title is available from the British Library

Trade Paperback ISBN 978 1 399 81574 1

ebook ISBN 978 1 399 81575 8

Typeset in Stone Serif ITC Pro 10.5/14.5 by Integra Software Services Pvt. Ltd., Pondicherry, India.

Printed and bound in Great Britain by Clays Ltd, Elcograf S.p.A.

John Murray Press policy is to use papers that are natural, renewable and recyclable products and made from wood grown in sustainable forests. The logging and manufacturing processes are expected to conform to the environmental regulations of the country of origin.

John Murray Press
Carmelite House
50 Victoria Embankment
London EC4Y 0DZ

www.sheldonpress.co.uk

John Murray Press, part of Hodder & Stoughton Limited
An Hachette UK company

Contents

Acknowledgements   vi

Foreword   vii

Introduction   xi

1   An age of anxiety – an age of opportunity *Kate O'Brien*   1
2   The Children's Fire: meaning and purpose *Mac Macartney*   10
3   Minding our (and their) emotions *Fiona Spargo-Mabbs*   24
4   Bridging the gap: using the African ethic of relatedness to unite generations *Dr Judy Blaine*   36
5   Learning in the age of distraction *Dr Karl Sebire*   49
6   Humanizing the classroom: lessons learned by a head of school *Mary Lyn Campbell*   61
7   Humanizing the workplace: living barefoot | The Vivo Way *Galahad Clark*   79
8   The house of tomorrow *Ed Olver*   86
9   Diving deep: my journey to self-discovery and Oceanic Global *Lea d'Auriol*   96
10   Courage: letters to humanity by father and daughter holders of contemporary wisdom *Mindahi and Xiye Bastida*   105
11   Finding myself: one breath at a time *Ryan Dusick*   115
12   Finding flow *Dr Easkey Britton*   120
13   Indigenous wisdom for troubled times *Tiokasin Ghosthorse*   126
14   The whole being *Cornelius O'Shaughnessy*   131
15   Nourishing body and mind *Charlotte Fraser*   147
16   Molly's story *Rachel Ollerenshaw*   168
17   Un:Stuck: flourishing *Kate O'Brien*   173
Appendix   Essential vitamin and mineral guide *Charlotte Fraser*   177

Further reading   186

Contributors   189

Index   195

Acknowledgements

I would like to thank everyone who helped bring these *Un:Stuck* stories to life, most of all the wonderful contributors who said a resounding 'yes' when invited to offer their expertise and wisdom to this book, with any fees donated to charity.

Also, thank you to the expert team at Sheldon Press in London, most especially Victoria Roddam and Alisha Raj.

A special thanks to my great friend Liz Remington, whose creative inspiration (and patience) helped cement the *Un:Stuck* title.

For my late husband, Mike, who encouraged me to fulfill my own dreams and who was always there to help me through uncertain times, but sadly is not around to read these *Un:Stuck* pages.

And for our children, Liam, Maya and Raif (these same young people featured in these pages) and for all the teens and young adults navigating their own futures. I hope these words from our collective will help them feel safe and loved so that they too can fulfill their wildest, deepest dreams.

Foreword

Firstly, I would like to congratulate all the contributors to this insightful and timely book. *Un:Stuck* is a gift to us all and an essential read for both older and younger generations.

'What makes you feel most alive?' Kate O'Brien asks in the introduction, as she outlines her personal reasons for bringing these pages to life. In this complex, rapidly changing world into which human children are born today, we know there is enormous suffering. And while there are myriad reasons for this, much of it is because our young people are not fully alive in their bodies, hearts and souls. No fault of their own, this is the consequence of a lack of authentic love, lack of meaning, lack of purpose and direction, with most young people today being pushed to seek success rather than personal fulfilment. Love of self, love of others and love of nature is the source of fulfilment, but many of us adults have taught our children to love money – and very little else. The importance of creativity and imagination is hardly highlighted in the classrooms, in homes or in the workplace now. If one is not clever enough to shine academically, then that young person is seen as a failure – hardly the recipe for developing well-rounded, balanced, happy and confident adults.

Wisdom arises when knowledge and experience meet, and *Un:Stuck* is the meeting place where these wise voices have come together in this timely manifesto for a more gentle, humanistic and integrated way of living.

As the founder of Schumacher College, education remains very close to my heart. I believe that the purpose of education is not to produce ever increasing numbers of consumers but to help humans become makers and creators, using their intuition and imagination as well as skill and technique. As former head of school, Mary Lyn Campbell, reminds us (Chapter 6), 'The sacred trust of educators is to ensure that young people are prepared and that they are well rounded, happy, responsible, capable and ready to do the right things, at the right time, for the right reasons.' In other words, education with hands, hearts and heads – and education where people and planet matter.

To make this happen, a shift is urgently needed – from information to knowledge, from seeing the world as a machine to understanding it as a network, from quantity to quality, from products to relationships. And most importantly, a shift from ego to eco: ego separates and eco connects. Ego complicates, eco simplifies. Eco means 'home', the place where relationships are nurtured, and it is our role as parents, teachers and providers of care for young people to create this home.

Everywhere we look and listen we are inundated with stories of war and hopelessness, but *Un:Stuck* reminds us of the kindness, joy and humanity that are right within our grasp, and through these pages we are invited to really feel into this by making some changes in our own lives, such as living more simply and seeing more deeply.

What is called *darshan* in Sanskrit could be translated as deep seeing – seeing that which lies beyond appearances. And this is what these wise, experienced contributors are offering – a deep insight into a better way of being in the world. To achieve this, we need to shut down our screens, then close our eyes, and visualize the wholeness of life and see with the eye of the heart that everything is interconnected, interrelated and interdependent. This, in my view, is the premise for *Un:Stuck*.

We all need money, but we need other things even more. We need a sense of belonging, a sense of community, a sense of mutuality and reciprocity; we need a sense of service and we need courage and confidence. Success is often measured in terms of money, but fulfilment is measured in terms of happiness. And happiness is one of the many outcomes of creativity. When I make something, be it writing a poem, painting a picture, planting a tree or cooking a meal for my friends, I feel happy. When I am walking in nature, watching birds or swimming in the sea, I feel happy. But our homes and schools undervalue these activities. Our one-dimensional mainstream culture promotes money and materialism, production and consumption. Yes, of course we need to earn money, but we also need to earn joy and learn to celebrate life. And this is the invitation offered in these pages.

Woven together like a colourful garland of fresh ideas and practical solutions, the collective contributions bridge the gap between generations, from older, wise indigenous elders, writers, academics and parents to younger activists, musicians and social scientists who, through unwavering passion and commitment, are rewriting storylines by empowering young people and guiding them towards fulfilling their deepest desires while also making the world be a better place.

In Chapter 10 Mindahi Bastida from the Otomi-Toltec Nation of Mexico writes, 'We have to go from the I to the We. From the Me to the We. It is the time. And that is the reason we are here.' The time is indeed now and I urge all readers to realize that essential balance between money and meaning, between having and being, between knowledge and wisdom, and most of all, I urge you to help and support our young people so they will flourish as they were born to do. The Further reading section at the end of the book includes many essential titles for all of us and I strongly advise you to take the time to read these.

All of this matters. It matters greatly and if we are to give this next chapter in our human story a fighting chance, together we must embrace our humanity and reach across the divide; we must listen well to our children; we must live lighter and live on less; and we must all take the pledge of The Children's Fire succinctly outlined by Mac Macartney (Chapter 2) as we begin our journey towards a deepening alignment with all of life.

Only then can we fulfil our vision for the world of tomorrow. We no longer have a choice.

Satish Kumar
Activist, founder of Schumacher College, Devon, UK, and editor emeritus of Resurgence & Ecologist *magazine*

Dawn Revisited

I sometimes forget
that I was created for Joy.
My mind is too busy.
My heart is too heavy
for me to remember
that I have been called to dance
the sacred dance of life.
I was created to smile,
To Love
To be lifted up
And to lift others up.

Hafiz, Persian poet (1325–90)

Introduction

Kate O'Brien

'Courage, dear heart.'

C. S. Lewis, *The Voyage of the* Dawn Treader

'What makes you feel most alive?' is the question I often ask my children. I am writing these words and bringing together these voices and stories for many reasons, but mostly because I know that many young people today have lost connection with the essence of what it means to be fully alive and this breaks my heart.

As the scaffolding of the old world has crumbled, everything we thought we knew is no longer, challenging how we as parents, teachers and providers have lived and led. Clinging to what used to be for too long, we are overwhelmed, technology rich but time poor, anxious to get everything right and fearful of the consequences of any tiny mistake we might make along the way. Our world is in pain. We are in pain and, fuelled by a collective deep sense of sadness and powerlessness, we are crying out for help.

Current statistics for youth mental health speak for themselves (see Chapter 1), as do the sadness, the fear, the loneliness and, for many young people, the anger that are ever present in their beautiful, vibrant young faces. For these teenagers and young adults, embracing their final school/college years and early working life through a screen at home was cruel and unnatural. Hardly surprising that college drop-out rates soared, along with rates of depression, anxiety, eating disorders, and other stress-related illnesses and suicidality.

Even pre-pandemic we were the loneliest humans in recent history. Our lives are full of 'stuff', but our lives are empty and hollow. Meaningful contact is something we are innately designed for. It is embedded in our DNA, yet loneliness hovers over our Western culture like a thick smog. As social psychologist Sherry Turkle, PhD, author of *Alone Together*, writes: 'Young people are more connected than ever before – yet they are alone together.'[1] She believes that an over-reliance on digital communication can result in feelings of real-world isolation and loneliness, emotional disconnection, anxiety and mental exhaustion.

We know the digital revolution has many benefits and that there is nothing inherently wrong with digital devices – it's their misuse that is of great concern. History has shown how it can take time for society to adjust to major changes and we need time to learn how best to maximize the many benefits of these technological advances. But our world is changing faster now than at any other time in our history – and keeping up is proving more difficult than we ever imagined. We have made mistakes and continue to do so. That said, we are human. We make decisions that we wish we could change in hindsight. But we also do so many things right in our own lives and in the lives of our children and others we connect with.

We know that many members of Gen Z (young people born 1997–2012) are suffering deeply with what Dr Lisa Miller, professor in the clinical psychology program at Columbia University, terms 'diseases of despair' – with anxiety, depression, addiction and even suicidality at epidemic levels. In her book *The Awakened Brain* she outlines how 25 years of hard research data are showing that having a spiritual core (or believing in some form of higher power) is the single most powerful factor for preventing these diseases of despair.[2] While the scientific findings are new, these inner spiritual paths have carried our ancestors through extremely challenging times in their own lives, but they are effectively lost to this generation.

Living as we have been with an enormous wisdom deficit we are paying the price in every area of our lives, most especially in the lives of the younger generation who are not being taught how to deal with their fluctuating emotions and with conflict and bullying, often until the consequences become extreme. 'Don't always look at the darkness in your experience, but look instead to see what grows from it – just as the lotus rises from the mud,' Cornelius O'Shaughnessy, a respected meditation, stress management and Eastern philosophy teacher, reminds us in Chapter 14. Weaving his personal story of rising from depression's murky waters to becoming *Un:Stuck*, he offers timely guidance to help others rise up and let their inner lights shine too.

Some years back, Australian psychologist and author Steve Biddulph said, 'Success, as defined by a glittering career, an affluent, busy lifestyle and outcompeting the other kids in your school, is a living nightmare. It's destroying the mental health of almost every boy and girl caught up in it. The sensitive, the open-hearted, the caring, the empathetic ones are the first to go. These are the sorts of people you need in society and they are the ones most battered by the world we live in.'[3] Recent years have only highlighted the relevance of this.

That said, our collective emphasis on nurturing positive mental health has led many to believe that feeling down is grounds for serious concern. As adults we know that life isn't perfect and that pain and suffering are inevitable. After all, *dukkha,* or suffering, is the first of Buddhism's Four Noble Truths. Many psychologists believe that we don't make enough room for sadness or grief in our world and that denying our pain only makes us harden with despondency and bitterness. Upset and disappointment are part of growing up and, as clinical psychologist and adjunct professor of psychology at University College Dublin, Tony Bates, writes in his book *Breaking the Heart Open*: 'Mental health is not about "feeling good" or "feeling bad"; mental health is about being connected with reality and with each other. It is about knowing how I am doing on any given day and asking myself: "What do I need?" "What might help?" "How much of this problem can I deal with now, and what do I leave for another time?"'[4]

I have been working and living in the wellbeing space for over 30 years and am an honours science graduate, qualified dietitian and yoga teacher, yet for a long time I felt powerless too, with few relevant books to call on for guidance. *Un:Stuck* is my timely way of opening the gateway to a brighter, richer landscape. Calling on my many years of professional experience and a deep network of wisdom holders and respected experts, each of whom views the world through a slightly different lens, we are coming together armed with a whole new deck of cards to guide us back to a more gentle, humanistic and integrated way of living.

Aside from my professional qualifications and experience, I am a mother of three adolescent and young-adult children and have witnessed first-hand how the past years have impacted my family's wellbeing. For some time I believed there was little I could do to help, bar keeping my children close through the constant challenges of daily life (albeit in pandemic crisis management mode!) Yet, the more I read about the chronic state of the global health system and the turmoil in our young people's lives, the more I despaired.

Then I read *Standing at the Edge: Finding freedom where fear and courage meet* by Buddhist teacher, social activist and founder of Upaya Zen Center in New Mexico, Roshi Joan Halifax, and something inside me tweaked with these words: 'To gain this balance and take action from a place of strength rather than fragility.'[5] I was fragile and I knew this was not helping anyone, least of all myself. She talks about 'edge states' being gateways to wider, richer internal and external landscapes. 'If we willingly investigate our difficulties, we can fold them into a view of reality that is more courageous, inclusive, emergent and wise,' she writes.

We know that young people today are angry and fearful and they know what they are angry about, often before they even know who they are. What if we, as parents, teachers and caregivers, were to truly listen, beyond the lip service we can be quick to offer? In a world where fear, apathy and powerlessness prevail, it is time to rethink the questions we ask our teenagers and young-adult children – and instead of advising them to choose a career where they begin that arduous climb to the top in a big multinational law firm or financial institution, we encourage them to consider more the challenges they wish to solve in the world and guide them towards fulfilling their desires, be it with a socially conscious legal or financial institution or elsewhere. After all, research is showing that it is the organizations that lead with purpose and impact that are changing the nature of business today. Just as ethical young activist Lea d'Auriol, founder of non-profit Oceanic Global, is doing. With a background rooted in loss, trauma, courage and self-discovery, she is rewriting storylines by empowering the leaders of tomorrow to turn their anger and despair into a clear vision for the future.

Through these pages we welcome in a world that advocates a life of greater thriving, health and belonging – one that can help us all, young and old, renew our relationship with one another, with the Earth and with life itself. It is because these ways have been lost that we are lost. Now it's time to walk each other home.

In Chapter 2, Mac Macartney, wisdom holder and founder of Embercombe in the UK, questions what it means to be human on this

Earth at this time: 'What is it that you love most deeply and profoundly? What are your deepest and most profound gifts? What are your deepest and most profound responsibilities?' he asks, as a way of helping young people interpret their place in the world. 'How can I place my roots so deeply into life that no matter how shocking the wind might blow, I will remain planted, knowing who I am and knowing what it is I should do?' Questions such as these are needed now more than ever. And *Un:Stuck* is the invitation.

Learning happens everywhere, most especially beyond the classroom, and our teachers are all around us – and they are inside us, nudging us along, minute by minute. Recently, during my early-morning meditation, I asked for guidance around a personal issue that had been bothering me for some time. I sat with myself and these words came to me: 'Be still and breathe ... it will be well.' Every morning I sit in stillness for a short while, and when I do, I know I'm in the right place for receiving support and direction. This hidden power is in each of us, yet many of us have not felt inclined to access it. For now, even if you have never done so before, please spend a few minutes in your own quiet space and visualize a world where you feel you have purpose and meaning – one where you feel optimistic and joyful for your own future, for that of your own children (if you have them) and family and the greater world. Just pause and sit with these feelings and let them stay with you.

Practices like this matter, and woven through these pages are simple exercises, prompts and real human stories to help you deal with sticky situations and fearful moments in your life and that of your children, students and clients. Just like the guidance offered by Irish surfer, author and marine scientist Easkey Britton. She draws on the power of our human connection with water to help restore a deeper connection within herself and with others and the wider world. 'Water acts as a powerful mirror,' she says. 'In it we see ourselves and are reminded of our capacity to be like water; of our remarkable potential to recover and return to wholeness; to move fluidly and find flow and to embrace the unknown.'

Others, like Ryan Dusick, founding drummer of the immensely successful Maroon 5, turned a decade of suffering into a new career as a mental health professional and author. 'The work I do now [as a therapist and author] has been equally, if not even more, fulfilling than creating music and performing,' he says. 'I am truly blessed to have found a second act in my life, but others may not be so lucky as anxiety, depression, addiction and other mental health challenges can lead to outcomes far worse than just losing your career as a performer.'

Being a qualified dietitian, a book written to help young people rise and flourish would not be complete without including pertinent nutrition advice for fuelling young bodies and minds. This vast subject is worthy of a book in itself, and while there are notable reads on the market, the ever-wise nutritional therapist Charlotte Fraser offers simple recommendations here for nurturing healthy young bodies and minds and for keeping essential brain neurons firing in sync and rewilding the health of our gut, which experts believe is the body's master controller – see Chapter 15 and Appendix.

We are all innately creative, but like us, our children are living too much in their heads. This new storyline offers fresh guidance to help break unhealthy patterns and nurture the resilience needed to navigate challenging times and the wisdom to feed the deep well of creativity that lies within us all. Through these pages we offer new ways of learning that will help ignite young people's curiosity and nurture confidence, tenacity and a real sense of interconnectedness, as echoed in the African ethic of holism, *Ukama*, succinctly captured by Dr Judy Blaine (Chapter 4).

In 'Humanizing the classroom' (Chapter 6), former head of school Mary Lyn Campbell recognizes that in this complex, rapidly changing world we must prepare children for situations that none of us could have anticipated and we must help them to redefine what it means to be a human being within their own historical context. 'If they have the emotional awareness and maturity, a social fabric on which to fall back when needed, and a real understanding of their own essence and spirit, what part of the future will they not then be prepared for?' she asks. 'The sacred trust of educators is to ensure they are prepared and that they are well rounded, happy, responsible, capable and ready to do the right things, at the right time, for the right reasons.'

Every day we are inundated with stories of rage, stories of divide and hopelessness, but we must balance these with other stories that focus on our kindness and humanity and remind us of the endless possibilities that often pass unnoticed. These are what we need to hear now. As best-selling writer and meditator Diego Perez (a.k.a. Yung Pueblo) says, 'A healing generation is happening quietly across the world, but the results of this will be extraordinary. Not only will the lives of individuals be improved, but this will impact the global collective.'[6]

Today's children and young adults are a new generation in a very different world. As parents, caregivers, teachers and guides we need to help them be brave enough to pave their own way, excited yet somewhat fearful and full of dogged hope for their future. To quote the late Sir Ken Robinson from his 2010 TED Talk, 'Bring on the learning revolution', 'We have to recognize that human flourishing is not a mechanical process; it's an organic process. And you cannot predict the outcome of human development. All you can do, like a farmer, is create the conditions under which they will begin to flourish.'[7]

When I am feeling a little fearful and wobbly myself, I seek time in nature, I sit in stillness and I often return to the words of author, social researcher and wise woman Brené Brown in her *Unlocking Us* podcast.[8] Brown, too, has a young adult daughter navigating grown-up life and she says that sometimes all she can offer her daughter are the words that she often whispers to herself: 'Strong back, soft front, wild heart.' She says these words breathe something into her that makes her 'kind of straighten up, take a deep breath and keep doing the next right thing'.

For our children to bravely grow into their true gifts they need this strong, courageous back to stand up for themselves, the soft front of compassion and vulnerability in the face of social media's callousness, and, most importantly, this wild heart overflowing with passion, joy and desire that will guide them towards fulfilling their sweetest dreams.

We want to help young people navigate this hugely challenging phase of their lives. We want to raise them to have rich and rewarding emotional lives and to feel safe and deeply loved – always. We want them to be able to access those gifts that are inside each and every one of them. These gifts are the tools that will help them lean into uncertainty and chaos with courage, knowledge and the strength to say what they truly believe without apology, to do what they feel is right, despite the fear of judgement and reprisal, and most of all to tune into the whispers of their wild hearts – as this new world needs their truth, their wildness and their tenacity, now.

One thing I wish someone had told me when I was on the cusp of adulthood was that everything I needed to get through my life – through my fears and self-doubts – was already within me. Speaking to that 18-year-old me now, I reassure her that she doesn't have to live up to her parents' or anyone else's expectations; she can pave her own footprints in the sand. Nor does she need to try to be anyone else but her beautiful, vibrant self. And when she does discover that which makes her feel most alive (and she will), she must nurture it with the inner force and dogged determination that has got her older self to where she is now!

I would also remind her that happiness and 'living her best life' are fleeting – they come and go – but meaning and purpose are what ultimately matter, while reminding her (yet again) to find a few moments of ease and stillness in her day, every day, so she can tune into the whispers of her vibrantly wild heart.

As parents, teachers and caregivers we must remember that we are not alone. These contributions from our collective are the very 'edge states' – the gateways to wider, richer internal and external landscapes that Roshi Joan Halifax speaks of. I hope they inspire you, and more than that, I hope that, wherever in our global village you call home, you will vow to engage and do more, as together we create the house of tomorrow (Chapter 8) and dream in a brighter, better world. Living on the cusp of this new way, it is today's Gen Z who get to experience how we will come together once again, how we will live and work, and who and how we will love. They, and those others coming after them, deserve the clearest and wisest direction possible.

To quote Julian of Norwich, English theologian and mystic (1343–1416): 'All shall be well. And all shall be well and all manner of things shall be well ... for there is a force of love moving through the universe that holds us fast and will never let us go.'

Notes

1   Turkle, Sherry, *Alone Together: Why we expect more from technology and less from each other*, 3rd edn. Basic Books, 2011.
2   Miller, Lisa, *The Awakened Brain: The psychology of spirituality and our search for meaning*. Penguin, 2021.
3   www.thetimes.co.uk/article/
    parenting-how-to-help-girls-grow-up-happy-kp5fb2wcf
4   Bates, Tony, *Breaking the Heart Open: The Shaping of a Psychologist*. Gill Books, 2023.
5   Halifax, Roshi Joan, *Standing at the Edge: Finding Freedom Where Fear and Courage Meet*. Flatiron Books, 2019.
6   https://yungpueblo.substack.com/p/the-healing-generation
7   www.ted.com/talks/
    sir_ken_robinson_how_to_escape_education_s_death_valley?language=en
8   Brown, Brené, *Unlocking Us* podcast.

1

An age of anxiety – an age of opportunity

Kate O'Brien

'Here is the world. Beautiful and terrifying things will happen. Do not be afraid.'

Frederick Buechner, writer and theologian

Every child is born an innately cognitive, physical, emotional and spiritual being – it is their birthright. As parents, teachers and providers it is our role to nurture these qualities and help young people mature into confident, embodied adults and responsible custodians of our communities, economies and the Earth.

We want our children to grow up in an environment where they feel safe and loved and can enjoy a deep sense of belonging, but there seem to be fewer institutions within our collective social, religious and political systems where they can feel that sense of trust and belonging. So much so that many reports have shown that we are the loneliest humans in history, as with the rise in technology and our subsequent disregard for the natural world, we have spent more time indoors, online, always doing, ever consuming and relentlessly chasing happiness and material success.

The recent pandemic years have been difficult for us all, most especially our younger generation. This is no fault of their own; they just happened to be approaching what should have been some of the most exciting years of their lives when the world they (and we) knew crumbled around all of us. With this, rates of depression, anxiety, eating disorders and other stress- and loneliness-related illnesses have dramatically escalated.

In 2021 the mental health status of youth in the USA was escalated to a national crisis by the US Surgeon General, Dr Vivek Murthy.[1] At the same time, a report by the Royal Pharmaceutical Society in the UK revealed that prescriptions for antidepressants among children aged

5–12 years had increased by more than 40 per cent between 2015 and 2021, while NHS figures in the UK showed a 28 per cent rise in children being referred to mental health services between April and December 2020.[2,3] Outcomes of studies carried out across the world during this period noted that symptoms of depression and anxiety among teens had doubled and that many young people started to have difficulty sleeping, withdrew from their families or became aggressive.[4,5]

Further reports by emergency medicine departments in the USA in early 2021 noted that visits for suspected suicide attempts increased by 51 per cent among teenage girls and by 4 per cent among teenage boys (compared with visits two years earlier), while the situation was worse for teenagers belonging to marginalized racial and ethnic groups.[6,7]

In Australia, the 2022 Australian Bureau of Statistics' National Health Survey revealed that close to 19 per cent of young people aged 15–24 reported feeling anxious, while 14 per cent experienced depression between 2020 and 2022.[8,9] In the UK, an estimated 7 per cent of children have attempted suicide by the age of 17, and a 2021 report in the *British Journal of Psychiatry* noted that almost one in four said they had self-harmed during that year.[10]

This said, even prior to the onset of the pandemic, alarms were being raised regarding child mental health, with UK-based child psychiatrist Sami Timini referring to escalating child psychiatric diagnoses and the rapid increase in the use of drugs to treat unwanted behaviour or emotions as the 'McDonaldization' of child mental health.[11] 'Perhaps the epidemic numbers of children in the West receiving diagnoses is a symptom not of something "wrong" that we should try to cure in the individual, but a barometer pointing to something "unhealthy" in the society, the culture that invented it,' he said.[12]

For many of today's young adults, fitting into a broken system was never going to work. Having come of age in the aftermath of 9/11 (the 11 September 2001 terrorist attacks in the USA), this young generation has witnessed climate and financial crises, technological disruptions, political extremism, mass shootings, and the toxic and devasting impact of social media, among other life-changing issues, all during their formative growing years.

Gun violence

In the years since the Columbine school shooting in Colorado (20 April 1999) when 15 people lost their lives, gun violence has continued to plague schools and colleges across the USA. Not all are mass shootings – some involve a single fatality – but all leave their scars firmly embedded in the children, teachers, parents and communities involved, with post-traumatic stress, anxiety and depression staying with these people for many years or whole lifetimes. Even now, the idea of being in a classroom can instil a sense of anxiety and fear in those involved. In a 2021 article titled 'The hidden costs of school shootings', American journalist Katherine Kam writes that 'since Columbine 256,000 children at 278 schools have been exposed to gun violence during school hours – a milestone of one-quarter million youths'.[13]

In a 2021 study, Maya Rossin-Slater, associate professor at the Stanford University School of Medicine, along with researchers at the University of Texas at Austin and Northwestern University in Evanston, Illinois, analysed 33 public schools in Texas where shootings had taken place between 1995 and 2016.[14] While not all of these involved fatalities, the study found that gun violence is costly in terms of children's mental health and their future educational and economic trajectories – while the mere exposure to shootings leads to a higher likelihood that children are absent from school, more likely to repeat a grade, less likely to graduate from high school, less likely to attend college and more likely to have lower earnings by their mid-twenties.

The smartphone and social media

Since the first iPhone launched in the USA in 2007 the smartphone has transformed many aspects of our lives. With everything we need now at our fingertips, daily life has become easier in so many ways. But the concurrent advent of social media in all its guises has left many of us, children in particular, prey to life-sucking content that nobody should ever see. While some young people appear to be able to better process what they are seeing and hearing, for the more sensitive and vulnerable in particular, every glance at Snapchat, TikTok, Instagram and so on hijacks their attention and dopamine reward systems, instilling repeated doses of envy, rejection and sadness and an overwhelming sense of unworthiness. Now, as research into the effect of smartphones on childhood and adolescent development continues to unfold we are being alerted to the dangers of these potentially disruptive technologies – with governments, schools and parents rising up in an unprecedented revolt against these Big Tech companies.

We know that the complex inner world of a teenager takes time, patience and a bucket load of compassion to understand (see Chapter 3, 'Minding our (and their) emotions'), and sadly too many of these young people do not have access to experienced experts to help them through this challenging time in their lives. With the constant pressures of trying to fit in with peer groups and on social media, and endlessly trying to achieve so they are good enough and worthy enough in their parents' eyes, self-harming has become an easy and viable coping mechanism. While intentionally injuring some part of their body by cutting, burning, head-banging, skin-picking and so on can temporarily relieve what for these young people is an overwhelming situation, when carried out regularly it becomes compulsive and can lead to more disturbing behaviours. So perilous is the crisis that the NHS in the UK reported that hospital admissions for self-harming had escalated by 22 per cent among children aged 8–17 within one year, with more than 25,000 hospital admissions countrywide noted at the end of March 2022 – the highest figure recorded for any age group.[15]

The pressure to succeed at a young age is overwhelming. As Mary Lyn Campbell, who has been on the frontline of educational leadership for over 35 years, writes in Chapter 6:

> For many of us working in education today, the main focus of what we do is directed towards academic rigor and achievement to the exclusion of almost all else. While well intentioned, the irony is that if we don't first build a solid relationship of trust and care with students, we inadvertently discourage them from reaching their fullest potential. And the idea that the school system (in response to parental and societal expectations) should dictate to young people who they have to be and what specific personal learning pathway they must follow, thereby denying their authentic voices, is worryingly unhealthy and unsustainable.

An epidemic of loneliness

While we know many aspects of the online world are worrying, one of the most concerning is the subsequent rise in loneliness – the prevalence of which has skyrocketed in recent years. Numerous reports in the USA indicate that about half of all adults have reported experiencing loneliness. In our frenetic world it is easy to forget that we humans are social animals, with a biological need for connection with others, and science has shown that it is that face-to-face connection that helps us feel loved and safe, giving us a real sense of belonging and safety that is impossible to find online.

Even before the pandemic we were ranked the loneliest humans ever. As social psychologist and author Sherry Turkle writes: 'As we ratchet up the volume and velocity of our [online] communication, we set up a pace that takes us away from each other.'[16] Turkle highlights that the impact of our over-reliance on digital communication can be felt most acutely among children who must compete with digital devices for direct eye contact with their parents when they come out of school or after-school activities. Turkle's research also shows that over-reliance on social technology may be causing us to become disconnected from our sense of self. 'It's a great psychological truth that if we don't teach our children how to be alone, they will always be lonely,' she adds, voicing her concern about how young people are losing touch with the realities of their physical surroundings and with the kind of solitude that refreshes and restores.

For many young people in particular the cascade of outcomes from overuse and misuse of social media – from a deeply engrained lack of self-esteem and feelings of worthlessness to relentless comparisons with others and a very real sense of helplessness – can alter their perception of themselves and the world around them, with serious impacts on essential daily activities like sleep, nourishment and in-person connection. So much so that it is not unusual to feel that our children are slipping from our adult grasp and becoming a sort of lost generation.

So urgent is the crisis that in May 2023 the US Surgeon General, Vivek Murthy, issued an advisory warning of the 'ample indicators' of the impact of social media having a 'profound risk of harm to the mental health and wellbeing of children and adolescents'.[17]

An age of opportunity

We know that this 'quick-fix-happy-meal' culture that Dr Sami Timini refers to is harming our children and our world. But perhaps this perfect storm could become the perfect opportunity, as we gently nudge humanity forward and pivot from the age of anxiety into an age of opportunity? To quote Viktor E. Frankl in *Man's Search for Meaning*, 'Everything can be taken from a man but one thing: the last of the human freedoms – to choose one's attitude in any given set of circumstances, to choose one's own way.'

In the face of the ongoing sadness, distress and bitter conflict in our world we know there is also great possibility. Our children will shepherd our future. We want to help them better navigate a challenging phase of their lives during this trying time in history. But what can we do? A lot, in short. Research and real-life experience show time and time again that given the right ongoing support, recovery from these diseases of despair that plague our youth is possible and indeed likely.

Further, we must remember that, regardless of our age, the human brain possesses neuroplasticity, a quality of being able to modify, learn and adapt throughout life and in response to experience. In other words, our brain is not fixed; it is malleable and continues to develop as a result of the events and behaviours we engage with through life. Like a muscle that grows more powerful, given the right instruction and encouragement our brain is capable of great change and can forge a clearer and better path forward.

A depth of research is now showing how a value-based system of learning in the classroom is helping educators provide young minds with a strong ethical foundation that will support them throughout their lives. By integrating a shared vocabulary based on common positive human values such as honesty, integrity, empathy, kindness or other similar values into the curriculum, students will learn at an early age how to take more responsibility for their learning and behaviour, how to develop critical thinking skills and how to better understand the consequences of their actions – in the playground, in the classroom and in life. For this to happen, teachers must be on board themselves by 'walking the talk' and living these values in their own lives – as this is how students learn best. And now as more schools are becoming responsive to mental health awareness and building emotional resilience in their students, there is further hope of healthier and happier outcomes. (See Chapter 6: 'Humanizing the classroom'.)

As these students progress into their professional lives, these very same values will stay with them in the workplace, despite the pressures to achieve targets and the focus on short-term gains. This approach goes well beyond simply imparting knowledge and skills – it moulds individuals who embrace social responsibility and strive for the betterment of themselves and society. (See Chapter 7, 'Humanizing the workplace', and Chapter 8, 'The house of tomorrow'.)

We know that, in the human and non-human mammal worlds, offspring respond to anxiety with parent-oriented attachment behaviours and that having loving parents close during anxious times can instantly calm a child's nervous system. So much so that research in the USA has found that, in some cases, simply shifting the focus of treatment from the child to their parents can help both parent and child better manage challenging situations and emotions.[18] Experts also believe that rather than trying to control certain negative behaviours in children, parents and providers should gently guide children towards more positive behaviours that might soon become normal practice.

We know that many of us are guilty of putting undue pressure on young people in our care to achieve what often surmounts to our version of 'success' through a cushy job and a certain level of income, or by living their 'best' life. While such pressure is often well intentioned, maybe it is time to take our foot off the accelerator so we can help them bring their passions and dreams to life in a positive and sustainable way.

Let us imagine our collective commitment to listening with open minds and open hearts to our children and those in our care. While for many of us it can be hard to take in other people's pain, frustration and loneliness, most especially those of our own children, when we do listen well, we realize that, although our life experiences and stages in life are vastly different, our hearts and desires are not, and letting them know that we hear and see them at every moment helps that resilience muscle grow stronger still.

To quote the 21st US Surgeon General, Dr Vivek Murthy:

> We have a choice right now between a world that is mired in fear, where people are angry at each other, where people are feeling left out, like they don't belong, like they'e on their own, where they feel invisible, and a world where people feel like they belong, where they have each others' backs, where they feel that the future is something that we can shape together, regardless of what may come, because we don't have to face it alone.
>
> So we've got to make that choice. Right now it seems the choice is being made for us – that we are steeped in this information environment that is extraordinarily negative – that's telling us that everything is broken about the world, that nobody can be trusted and that everyone is only out for themselves. We've got to turn that off and tune in to what's actually happening in our communities and choose again, love.
>
> I always say that with every decision we make, we can ask ourselves a question: am I making this decision out of love or out of fear? And if we choose love as often as we can, then we will build the kind of life that feels good for us, that's good for our communities, one that our kids can be proud of and that will help create the world that ultimately future generations need.[19]

Our children are watching our behaviour and how we choose to act in this world reminds them of a better way. As Fiona Spargo-Mabbs writes in Chapter 3, '[as parents and providers] the ball always starts in our court, because we are the grown-ups. It's up to us to pick up the pieces and go back to our teen, and let them know that they are safe, and loved, and always will be, however that translates itself into the needs of a particular moment.'

Let's come together to help young people find their way. Let's be there for them as they forge a deeper connection with their intuition, their emotional intelligence and inner knowingness, so that even the most troubled teenagers can call on their innate intelligence to ride their fears, speak their truth, better understand their sexuality, all with the unwavering courage to fulfil the vision that is intuitively theirs. After all, we all need to know we are seen and understood. We need to know that we matter.

Notes

1. https://www.hhs.gov/about/news/2021/12/07/us-surgeon-general-issues-advisory-on-youth-mental-health-crisis-further-exposed-by-covid-19-pandemic.html
2. https://pharmaceutical-journal.com/article/news/number-of-young-children-prescribed-antidepressants-has-risen-by-41-since-2015
3. Donnelly, Laura, 'Number of children taking antidepressants hits all-time peak during pandemic', *Telegraph*, 24 June 2021.
4. https://pubmed.ncbi.nlm.nih.gov/34369987/
5. https://mottpoll.org/reports/how-pandemic-has-impacted-teen-mental-health
6. https://pubmed.ncbi.nlm.nih.gov/34138833/
7. https://pubmed.ncbi.nlm.nih.gov/34608463/
8. https://www.theguardian.com/society/2022/mar/21/mental-health-issues-more-common-among-young-australians-national-survey-suggests
9. Australian Bureau of Statistics, Causes of Death, Australia, 2019.
10. Patalay, Praveetha and Fitzimons, Emla, 'Psychological distress, self-harm and attempted suicide in UK 17-year olds: Prevalence and sociodemo-graphic', *British Journal of Psychiatry*, 219(2), August 2021.
11. Timini, Sami, 'The McDonaldization of childhood: Children's mental health in neo-liberal market cultures', *Transcultural Psychiatry*, 47(5), November 2010.
12. Timini, Sami, *A Straight Talking Introduction to Children's Mental Health Problems* 2nd edn. PCCS Books, 2020.
13. https://katherinekam.com/2021/09/10/the-hidden-costs-of-school-shootings/
14. https://healthpolicy.fsi.stanford.edu/news/new-study-gun-violence-schools-identifies-long-term-harms-0
15. https://www.bbc.com/news/uk-england-64874355
16. https://www.apa.org/education-career/guide/paths/sherry-turkle
17. https://www.hhs.gov/about/news/2023/05/23/surgeon-general-issues-new-advisory-about-effects-social-media-use-has-youth-mental-health.html
18. https://www.jaacap.org/article/S0890-8567(19)30173-X/fulltext
19. https://www.richroll.com/podcast/surgeon-general-783/

2

The Children's Fire: meaning and purpose

Mac Macartney

'He who has a why to live for can bear almost any how.'

Friedrich Nietzsche[1]

In 2017 my son, Cai, was born. That morning I held him in my arms for the first time, and old enough to be his grandfather, I had yet another deep experience of this mysterious phenomenon we call love. Wrapped in a small, fleecy blanket, with his mother's eyes softly watching, I whispered, 'He is beautiful.' Now, six years on, he has recently made his first longbow, competes with me in playing darts and basketball, wrestles, rides bareback the wild assertions of his emotions, and boisterously lets us all know that he is most profoundly and, in his view, uniquely alive. His brother, Kevo, 18 years his senior, his mother, Wandia, and I, we are all at times variously exasperated, inspired, enchanted, angry, bemused, amused and bewildered by this latest addition to our warm, noisy and strangely delightful family. I am a man blessed in many ways.

On a number of occasions in conversation with others I have encountered people who have chosen not to have children in the belief and conviction that the future is hostile, bleak and probably brief. For them the question 'Why would you voluntarily bring a new life into a world that is so fixated upon a story that places greed, egotism, selfishness, power and the short term ahead of all other considerations?' is paramount. Our world is at once a dominant human culture that appears to loathe beauty, despise nature and almost exclusively measure success in terms of fame, wealth, power and influence. A world whose prevailing culture chooses to ignore the now well-researched and manifestly clear prediction that if collectively we do not choose to embrace radical change in the way we live upon this Earth we will rob our children of that which we have so carelessly enjoyed – the Eden into which we were born – a world we have so single-mindedly ravished, poisoned, plundered and broken.

This is worth some pause for thought.

However, when I looked into Cai's eyes on that first day of his life I saw, and more importantly felt, the fierce, unfathomable furnace of creation's desire to exist and be seen. From the very beginning it has always been so.

Walking along the lane that traverses the village of Ashton on the hills above the Teign river in Devon, you pass many desirable properties. They are expensive homes, mostly purchased by people who have garnered their wealth elsewhere before moving into the villages and settling into the comfort, quiet and security of one of the UK's safest rural localities.

Were we able to go back a few centuries, what would we see? Small, damp, dark, draughty houses and huts, many suggesting the poverty of the residents. Occasional epidemics and famine, precarious employment, no basic pension, rough justice, servitude, conscription, racial intolerance and the subjugation of women were all familiar to Ashton's residents back then. In addition, the village population was always vulnerable to the whims and traditions of feudal landowners and gentry who were supported in their right to power and privilege by both church and state.

Lives were shorter and much more physically painful back then. The freedoms and rights we enjoy today have been hard won and often fiercely resisted. The lives of our ancestors from the Bronze Age to the middle of the twentieth century will have felt as precarious, uncertain and fraught as the future seems to us now. Yet life went on and babies continued to be born.

In truth, regardless of how painful and challenging life is, most people will continue to choose life even when there is little hope of better times ahead. Like the young of all species, they cling to life, prepared to take their chances for the future when the tough times come.

Even now, at six years old, my young son perceives meaning and purpose in his life. He looks to his mother and father for affirmation that his life matters, that he is loved and that he belongs. He has already absorbed the fact that both his parents are engaged in activities that seek to benefit others while also serving the needs of the family. In his own way he is reaching for a vision of what his life might mean, of how he might achieve self-respect and self-authority and be taken seriously. Cai would be outraged if I ever suggested that it might have been kinder never to have enabled his chance of life. Even at six years old I know this to be true of him.

Much like what Yuval Noah Harari describes in his book *Sapiens: A Brief History of Humankind*,[2] I believe that human beings are born before being fully ready. Unlike the baby deer, fox or badger, we need years of care before we are able to successfully fend for ourselves. The plasticity of our minds and emotions as children means that, while we have the ability to learn very well, we are immensely dependent on the quality of the environment and influences that inform that learning. We have the potential to become kind, responsible, generous, courageous, discerning and knowledgeable. And we also have the potential to become cruel, traumatized, insecure and dangerously aggressive. The society into which most human children are born does not seek to develop well-rounded, balanced, happy, confident people; instead it hurls them into a world that is driven by a marketplace serving the crudest measure of success: economic growth.

In the absence of a culture that celebrates and respects life, and cares so little for the future welfare of our own species, let alone that of others, this immense challenge now squats before every adult that takes a different view. Parents and teachers stand at the forefront, but countless others stand alongside. We have to be brave and we have to prevail. And this all begins with questions relating to meaning and purpose.

'What is the purpose of a human life?' asks the Indigenous elder. I listen. 'To care for all living things – what else?' What brings joy to the human heart? I ask myself. 'Being in service to a way of living that serves the greater good, both human and more than human,' I reply softly to myself. Our species possesses extraordinary gifts and powers, but, as with all else, the question remains the same: to what end are these capabilities given?

It seems that for our cleverness to be an asset that can be trusted, it is imperative that at a species level we commit to a shared sense of purpose. Meaning is revealed to us when we remember that we are part of nature and part of the living Earth. Stories and ideologies that elevate us to some kind of pre-eminence, that adorn us with the qualities and rights of deities, and that separate us from all other forms of life, are at best unhelpful and usually dangerous. They lead to separation, hubris and eventually madness. This is where we are now. Our species shows every sign of mental illness, an obsession with our own greatness and manifest destiny. A narcissistic pathology that unhindered will take us to the cliff edge, along with the wider family of more-than-human relatives whom we have so resolutely shunned and exploited over this last couple of thousand years.

Where do we look for inspiration? Where can we find the trailing threads of a different worldview that might lead us home to our wider plant, animal and mineral family? What is the therapy that might soften our hearts, enable our imagination to take wing and set us homeward bound? Answers to these and similar questions have been forever extended to us by the outstretched hands of Indigenous cultures that still adhere to ways of living that honour our Earth, comprehend interdependence, practise regenerative ways of living, and know that to be whole we must embrace the physical, emotional, mental and spiritual. A worldview that encompasses spirituality invites us to behold the world in which we are privileged to briefly live with gratitude, reverence, reciprocity and wonderment. A world that speaks to us of beauty, responsibility, care, courage, kindness and inclusivity – a society and culture brimming with meaning and in which purpose is found in the warp and weft of the cloth that is a life well lived.

The Children's Fire

Here is a principle that I believe might draw us back from the cliff edge. A principle which if expressed in action might invigorate the way we, and all human systems upon this Earth, live. The Children's Fire is a story, a fragment of ancient wisdom, a longing and a way of thinking and perceiving. I have shared this story numerous times over many years and in many different ways. I was told that the wisdom offered in the story fell by the wayside a long time ago. If so, the consequences of this careless dereliction of duty have cost us dearly.

I was introduced to The Children's Fire in 1984. It was a wintery night in the coastal mountains of northern California. I sat by a blazing fire in a forest glade. I was tense, alert and mindful that every word, gesture and glance was significant. Even though I had no way of knowing the extent to which this brief encounter would influence the rest of my life, I experienced it as a tryst to which all roads had been leading even before I had learned how to walk. Since that time, The Children's Fire has become the cornerstone of my thinking about leadership, about life and about living.

I was told a story. I was told that this story was true, but to date all my efforts to research the origins of The Children's Fire and establish the veracity of its lineage have proved unfruitful. Currently I am inclined towards the conclusion that, unlike the Haudenosaunee Seven Generations Principle,[3] The Children's Fire originated in the mind and imagination of an inspired individual who later pretended an ancient Indigenous lineage to give it gravitas and authority. If so, and I may be wrong of course, then the wisdom of this simple yet profound idea was partially disabled by the lie that accompanied its birth.

The idea informing this story is powerful, enduring, contemporary and an open challenge to all who spare a thought for tomorrow. For this reason, whether carrying a lineage of hundreds or thousands of years, or a much shorter time span, I offer this because it has informed and continues to inform all aspects of my own life and those of others who are a part of my life and community.

The Children's Fire goes like this:

A long time ago the elders of the people would sit together in council and many questions important to the wellbeing of the tribe were discussed. A recurring question concerning the nature of leadership and the wielding of power was this: 'How shall we govern our people?'

One of the great challenges which the elders considered was the complex relationship between the short and the long term. It was understood that actions which yield short-term benefits may not always serve the tribe's best interests in the long term. As with all of their animal relatives they understood that children were their most important investment and the tribe's future. This naturally led them to understand the necessity of ensuring that their leaders always sought to secure a safe and prosperous future by testing every major decision against the ongoing wellbeing of the children.

In the culture from which The Children's Fire is believed to have emerged, everything physical was an expression of the invisible spiritual life force flowing within it, existing in a world of living symbols, each one a clue to the spiritual power that charged it. The chiefs ordered that a small fire be kindled in the centre of their council circle. This small fire was called The Children's Fire. It was located in the centre of the council circle to remind the chiefs of the first law:

> No law, no decision, no action, nothing of any kind will be permitted to go out from this council of chiefs that will harm the children.

Each chief was required to pledge themselves to The Children's Fire. It was on this condition that they took their seat on the council.

The Children's Fire is a pledge to the welfare of born and unborn children (human and more-than-human alike), but more profoundly it is a promise or vow to life, a commitment to the responsibility carried by each successive generation to safeguard the vitality and regenerative capacity of the Earth. It insists on a circular economy and it views any action that compromises the extravaganza of beauty from which our species has emerged as sacrilege, an act of betrayal and evidence hinting at insanity.

The Children's Fire is a regenerative principle, a lodestar guiding the deliberations of leaders who are charged with the responsibility of governance and the long-term welfare of their people – the same meaning we ascribe to the concept of sustainability. It is a mindset, a design principle that must one day find a home in our hearts, somewhere deep within the fabric of our homes, politics, religion, art, business, education, health, banking, cities. Everywhere.

The Children's Fire speaks to us about the wielding of power and authority, and the tendency for adults to forget their obligations and responsibilities and use all or most opportunities to feather their own nest. John Dalberg-Acton's phrase 'Power tends to corrupt, absolute power corrupts absolutely. Great men are almost always bad men' comes to mind. The Children's Fire is an attempt to protect against this gross human failing.

The Children's Fire burning at the centre of the council circle also represents our relationship to the Sun. Like the planets orbiting around the great fire at the centre of our solar system – the Sun – we acknowledge the star whose heat still pulses beneath our feet at the centre of the Earth and in the heat of our bodies and the fire of our imagination. The

Children's Fire represents sacredness at the centre of all that there is. The Children's Fire implies living in an animate world where everything is alive and everything has significance. An immanent world, in which gratitude and reverence become integral to everyday living.

The Children's Fire reminds us of a spiritual truth that needs to be followed if we are to be resilient and flourish over the long term. It doesn't ask people to *believe* in anything, but rather to simply acknowledge the insight and wisdom that it speaks of and then apply the principles in action. It is pragmatic.

The Children's Fire invites us to be the best we can be. It is an invitation to a lifetime journey of deepening alignment with life. It sets us a challenge and invites us to walk in beauty, to participate generously, to appreciate the inner journey as much as the outer, and it defines value in terms of what we give, not what we pretend to own.

In truth, The Children's Fire is simple common sense – a statement of the blindingly obvious – which is at least partly why its absence from almost all institutions administering power is so radically bewildering. Government, board rooms, churches, prisons, universities, public services, schools and not least families would all be better served by adopting the principle and practice of The Children's Fire.

If meaning speaks to the eyes with which we perceive the world, the stories we tell ourselves and how we interpret our place in the world, then purpose is how we choose to respond. There are three questions that I believe are helpful in finding our purpose:

1 'What is it that I most deeply and profoundly love?'
Before answering, it is essential that the full weight of our consideration dwells on the words 'deeply and profoundly'. This question, and indeed each of the three, does not ask for a few moments of reflection but rather a lifetime of enquiry that accompanies us as we traverse the various stages of life. Were I to have asked this question of my teenage self I might have heard a very different answer from that from the man I am now. My six-year-old son would answer the question in an age-appropriate manner. The experience of our lives will shape the answer and very often imminent death will provide a portal within which what was once opaque swiftly becomes clear.

Some years ago I was invited to join a gathering by the World Wildlife Fund (WWF) and spend a few days with the top-performing

European senior sales team of a multinational retail business. The global sustainability director was hoping, that by convincing this group to commit to the ethos and practice of sustainability, many others within the business would follow suit. The science and economics supporting the necessity of making this change were compelling, unequivocal and authoritative. The executives were bored, indifferent and unconvinced. During a break prior to one of the last sessions, and knowing that the seminar was heading towards certain failure, a short meeting was convened to ask if there was anything further we could do.

As a last resort, we adopted a different strategy... As the group of executives gathered for the final session, I asked them to sit in a circle and said that I would like each of them to answer a question. But before knowing what the question was, I asked them to promise that they would answer courageously and truthfully. It was, in effect, a dare. They responded very positively. The room was quiet as they waited for the question: 'What is it that you (personally) most deeply and profoundly love?'

There was a groan and a shifting of feet. I reminded them of the promise they had made. They quietened again. The person I asked to answer first was someone I felt I could trust to genuinely dive deep and set the tone for the others (which was just what they did). A short while later the meeting was paused. The first tears had been shed by the third speaker and from then on the depth of emotion became so visceral, noisy and powerful that all of us were deeply affected. During the break I had to attend to one of the directors who was weeping uncontrollably. After some time we reconvened and the atmosphere remained intense, compassionate, intimate and trusting.

What did they speak of that impacted everyone present so greatly? They spoke of their children, partners and families, of beautiful landscapes and places in nature, of hopes and sometimes fears, of communities and of music. They spoke of everything that makes human beings happy, content, secure and imaginatively engaged. They spoke of meaning and purpose.

They spoke of tenderness, mountains, forests, the seashore and meals shared with loved ones as the sun set over azure seas, or wrapped in the cosy warmth of a family home with laughter, silliness and deep affection, hugging all close in bonds of friendship and love. They spoke

17

of lives well lived in a peaceful, beautiful and companionable world, just as I knew they would once they were willing to engage with the question.

After another short break, I responded:

> For two days you have dismissed everything we brought you, everything showing that business as normal will ultimately and inevitably collapse the future and bring great distress to many. You asserted that none of this had anything to do with you because your task was to sell and get the company's products flying off the shelves of countless retail outlets. You scorned the concept of sustainability and saw no relationship or relevance to yourselves. Yet now, in answering this particular question, you have named all those elements of your respective lives that are, in effect, sacred and that bring you joy and a sense of belonging and meaning. Those things you spoke of are those same things we spoke of in the preceding presentations. And what you have told me you love is what the principles of sustainability are seeking to protect.

The gathering concluded with this group of executives committing their teams to a range of initiatives that would fundamentally change the way they did business – in essence, one small step towards the world we all want. Together with the other consultants and the WWF team, we withdrew. I never found out what eventually transpired, but as I have been in similar situations many times since, I offer this hypothesis: this senior team left the seminar determined to fulfil the commitments they had made. However, the demands that targets, budgets and career aspirations uphold remained in place and within a relatively short time a new chief executive probably took over and the shareholders, ever watchful, demanded their dues. The weight of the status quo no doubt allowed some progress, which would have been diluted by the ever-increasing volume of goods sourced, scaled and sold. And measured against the overwhelming requirement for radical action, I suspect that life fairly swiftly returned to incremental and wholly insufficient changes in business methods and practice.

In the same way that we have 'fair trade' goods, and what this then suggests about all the other products that don't qualify, we also have social enterprises and, conversely, businesses that are almost exclusively driven by growth, profit and shareholder value.

In a world that would rediscover meaning and purpose, every business would be first and foremost a social enterprise. Why not? When we uncover what it is that we most deeply and profoundly love, we have in a sense defined what is sacred to us. To betray this knowledge would be deeply saddening and would leave us all irretrievably weakened – unless of course, like the wild salmon, we swam all the way back upstream and knelt at the altar of our own self-respect.

I have brought this question to countless people, individually and in large gatherings. And on those occasions when I have had the privilege of working with people in some depth, I have often met the following answer to my question:

'I never have.'

'You never have what...?' I asked.

'Loved... deeply and profoundly,' they replied.

These words take us to the dark and unfathomed depths that many of us do everything we can to conceal. The loneliness that walks alongside this realization is palpable and it hurts deeply. I do not and perhaps never will understand why a question such as this is not asked and discussed repeatedly throughout the education of our children and young people. The very same question should resurface throughout our adult lives. Love is at the basis of everything that makes a human life bearable and potentially joyful. An embodied knowing of the sacred begins with experiences which teach us about love and loving. When we know what we love, *deeply and profoundly*, we know what it is to which our lives must be given in service. It is because I hold the answer to this question deep within my heart that my own life has become so rich, textured and fulfilling.

Knowing what we love does not mean we won't feel pain and grief. In fact, it probably means that we will feel pain and emotion ever more intensely because we only have to open our eyes, ears and hearts to behold the immense suffering endured by so many people, creatures of all kinds, trees, plants and habitats. Knowing what we love is to know beyond the shadow of a doubt that the collateral damage incurred by the way we do civilization is vast, unremitting and merciless.

2 'What are your deepest and most profound gifts?'

This question makes an assumption that might make some of us deeply uncomfortable. It assumes that we each have a gift which runs contrary to the conviction of many people. We may be aware of our qualifications and experiences, and we may carry a title which infers some level of competence, but *gifts*...?

Elders of a culture very different from my own once said to me that when a child is in its mother's womb, creation whispers to the unborn child: 'I am going to give you a gift. A little piece of my genius. I am going to hide this gift deep inside your gut. Upon being born your task is to locate this gift, grow it, bring it to fullness and then forever share it.'

I like to imagine this second question also accompanying our children throughout their education. I like to imagine it as their companion throughout life and for all time. If, within every school, the teaching staff made the same assumption and understood that it was their responsibility to support each child in knowing that they carry a unique gift and to assist them in revealing it and finding expression, I wonder what the outcome might be? I think we would see a measurable rise in the self-worth of many young people who have failed academically or who believe themselves to have done so. I also believe that many young people who possess outstanding academic grades also carry a deep and enduring sense of worthlessness. Coming to the realization of our gifts does not of itself make everything okay, but it does help. It helps a lot.

Our true gifts speak to us of the work we should do during our adult lives and our careers, as it were. I recollect that my one single meeting with the careers advice teacher in my school was gloomy and unpromising. Estate agency was fleetingly mentioned, physical education, the Church of England, or – my mother's suggestion – the circus! I opted for physical education because I was good at sport and liked being outdoors, but mostly because it temporarily solved the problem of what I should do with my life in the following years! In the end, however, my interest waned and I followed the faint traces of a hidden pathway that to this day I believe life lobbed at me as a kind of lifebuoy. Coming close to drowning a few times, I did eventually make it to shore...

Looking back, I recall arriving at boarding school when I was nine years old. I was naive, friendly and easy-going. I imagined that the experience would be mostly fun. I arrived a term later than the other new children and was therefore the only new child in the dormitory. As we all climbed into our beds and the lights were turned out, I remember the insinuating fear that consumed my small body. I remember the palpable hostility of the silence and the sudden realization that an attack was imminent. Out of the darkness came a disembodied voice:

'So, new boy, what's your story?'

I understood that this was a prelude to violence. In my fear and out from nowhere, I answered.

'I was born in Africa, deep in the bush. Wild animals were my friends and many times I came close to losing my life.'

No one was more surprised than me. I gulped. I was committed. There was no turning back. And so, I told a story, a story rich in narrow escapes, strange powers, bare fangs and titanic feats of strength. I waxed lyrical, and sensing that the hostility in the room was dissipating, I forged on. Night after night for a whole term I told tales of my fictitious childhood. The stories unashamedly plagiarized the works of Rudyard Kipling, Edgar Rice Burroughs and Arthur Conan Doyle, enthusiastically infiltrated with fantasies of my own and the little I knew of Davy Crockett and Robin Hood. The attacks never came. I found my feet in this new school, but while I survived, I don't think I thrived.

It was decades later, when faced with my indigenous mentors' challenge to speak publicly on behalf of our Mother Earth, that I eventually disinterred this gift. It took some time to dust it off, take the plunge and risk humiliation, but now speaking and using story are gifts that I deploy in almost all my work.

Just because we are frightened of something does not mean that it isn't a gift. Indeed, perhaps we are frightened of it because it is a gift. A gift that calls us to become visible and show ourselves to a world yet to be convinced. Our gifts should always be given in service to that which we love. Allowing our gifts to be the central pillar around which our careers pivot is about as close as we can get to ensuring success. Becoming successful, we shine and feel good about ourselves, and the world responds in small and occasionally bigger ways by offering rewards. I have learned that being in service to that which we love through the use of our gifts benefits both ourselves and all else.

Last comes the third and final question which sobers the exuberance of the previous two.

3 **'What are your deepest and most profound responsibilities?'**

Love, gifts and responsibilities – three questions to guide a journey. Easy to speak, more difficult to live, and yet they guide us to the way of being that so many speak of yet so few enjoy: happiness.

Happiness flows when we follow the original instructions that accompanied human beings onto this Earth: know gratitude, tend and care for all living things, learn and grow towards the goal of wholeness. Eschew perfection – it's a childish fantasy. Love the experience of living on this Earth. It is a privilege and available for only a short time. Be generous, kind, forgiving, and don't forget to dance and sing. If the Earth is a garden, we should seek to leave it more beautiful than we found it.

Without it necessarily being made explicit, our society tends towards the suggestion that our responsibilities should be few and mostly self-serving. There are many whose lives are given towards the cause of changing the self-destructive trajectory upon which we have become entrenched, while there are many others who could be persuaded to join this movement. Measured against the active and passive resistance to the social and environmental imperatives demanding change, so far these efforts show no likelihood of being ultimately successful. Our preferred interpretation of responsibility constrains itself to our personal ambitions and desires, with no serious challenge from within the establishment to the hegemony of private and corporate wealth, greed and power.

The Children's Fire principle does not limit itself to my children, nor does it limit itself to the young of my species. It spreads its arms far and wide and speaks of a reciprocal relationship with life. My responsibilities do not shrink when confronted with national borders, peoples of different religion or culture, oceans I may never swim in, or wild places I will only ever see as images on a page or screen or in my imagination. I know that my responsibilities include the absolute requirement to act upon the answers emerging from the first two questions and then throw my arms around the local and far-flung regions that describe the known world.

If we are to give this human story another chapter, we cannot hide behind illusionary boundaries. We have to reach across the divide, build bridges, focus more attention on listening and building empathy. We have to embrace our humanity and take a seat in the wide, wide council of all living things along with the trees, the rivers, the gardens, the soil... the Everything. In this widest circle of life, while always attending to what is under our feet and in our immediate locale, we must remember that we are family, we are related and we belong with one another.

Standing before the young, the born and the unborn, my children, your children and all the wild beings of our beautiful Earth, I will not hide from the size of the challenges rising before me. It does not serve us to calculate the chances of success, or rest upon vague hopes that somehow, magically, everything will turn out fine. We have to hold the hands of all whom we love, reach for those unknown others who could be friends and allies, befriend our enemies and be resolute in taking the pledge of The Children's Fire. If we do this, we have done all we can and our lives will count for something. In the words of Edward Everett Hale:

> I am only one, but I am one. I cannot do everything but I can do something. And because I cannot do everything, I will not refuse to the something that I can do.[5]

Notes

1. Nietzsche, Friedrich, 'Maxims and Arrows', Maxim 12, *Die Götzen-Dämmerung – Twilight of the Idols.* Penguin Classics, 1990.
2. Harari, Yuval Noah, *Sapiens: A brief history of humankind.* Vintage, 2015.
3. The Haudenosaunee confederacy from which came the Great Law of Peace, and within this the Seven Generations Principle. This advises on the wisdom of considering the impact of any decision on those born seven generations hence.
4. Dalberg, John-Acton in a letter to Bishop Creighton on 5 April 1887. John Neville Figgis and Reginald Vere Laurence (eds), *John Emerich Edward Dalberg-Acton.* Macmillan, 1907.
5. Hale, Edward Everett in Edwin Osgood Grover, *The Book of Good Cheer: A little bundle of cheery thoughts*, 1909, p. 28.

3

Minding our (and their) emotions

Fiona Spargo-Mabbs

In Blackwater Woods, New and Selected Poems, Volume One

'To live in this world
you must be able
to do three things:
to love what is mortal;
to hold it
against your bones knowing
your own life depends on it;
and, when the time comes to let it go,
to let it go.'

Mary Oliver, in Blackwater Woods

The world is a very different place for teenagers now than it was when their parents were teenagers. That's a truth so obvious it hardly needs telling, but it's easy to forget quite how much impact this has had, for good and sometimes not so good. When I myself was 16, back in the 1980s, a fourth television channel had not long joined the only three previously available. A telephone was generally wired to a wall in the hall, kitchen or living room. To find out something you had to go to the library. I'd been offered (and tried) alcohol and offered (and not tried) cigarettes, but I'd never seen an illegal drug and didn't know anyone that had.

By the time my younger son, Dan, was 16, the online world had emerged and already transformed the landscape of the average teenager, both inside and out, almost beyond recognition. It meant Dan and his friends (without me knowing about anything other than the party nearby he'd asked permission to go to) could message one another online to meet, find their way to an illegal rave that had been organized through social media, and on the way there take a drug I'd never heard of, which was easily available by messaging a dealer and affordable with a bunch of boys' paper-round and pocket money. Dan died three days later from multiple organ failure caused by MDMA toxicity. We spent those days by his side in intensive care, willing him to live yet watching him die, and wondering how this could have happened to our bright, big-hearted boy.

And so my new journey began, and here I am ten years on, heading up a leading drug education charity, working as hard as I possibly can to prevent harm happening to anyone else's child. There has been a lot of learning along the way, not just about drugs and drug education but also about the wonderful, bewildering, tumultuous world of the adolescent head and heart.

As an English teacher and manager in adult education for many years, I already knew a great deal about what makes teaching and learning work, and I knew a great deal in particular about the important role parents and carers play in children's learning and development because that had become my specialism. This involved working closely with schools and early years settings, all on the basis that parents, carers and teachers between them can make a world of difference to children and young people's learning, and, of course, to their lives.

Starting from there, to setting up a drug education charity, driven by the needless loss of my own dear Dan, at the heart of it all has always been equipping all those significant adults in young people's lives with all that I wish I'd known myself before Dan died. All that might, perhaps, have brought Dan home safely that night. Hence my first book for parents and carers, *I Wish I'd Known – young people, drugs and decisions*, in 2021. But while it's easy to feel lost and helpless in the face of vast territories of ignorance about our teenagers' world, and incapable of guiding them safely across such unfamiliar terrain, there's a lot we do know and a lot we can do – and this is a lot of the most important stuff.

Although young people now have a wide world of information and communication at their fingertips, on the phones in their pockets, and can be exposed at the touch of a screen to images, ideas, influences and avenues of opportunity, nevertheless the essential core ingredients of the average teenage experience remain broadly the same. Those very same physiological, neurological, social and emotional developmental stages of growing up that happened to us happen in much the same way for our children. And fundamentally, within this different world, every one of them still needs to know that they are always and forever loved, that they are listened to and safe, and that they have value and a validated place in a world in which they are emerging as increasingly independent beings.

However, the important question remains: am I okay? And as parents, carers, practitioners and educators we can do a lot about that, even though we may not ever quite be able to keep up with the rapidly changing, fluid online and real-life experience of a child and young person today. Connection and communication are key, and small and simple in both can make the world of difference, if and when big and complicated come into play. Being around, being available, being attentive and really, honestly, genuinely listening, and making sure children and young people always know you are always there for them, and always on their side, and always, always loving them more than they can possibly imagine. How we go about this will need to undergo a process of transformation, however. Our important, ongoing project is to work out how to evolve our parenting from child, to teen, to young adult and beyond.

What, how and when

It takes roughly 15 years to transform a child into a fully fledged adult. There is so much going on socially, emotionally, cognitively and physically during this time that can take both the child and their parents by surprise throughout these years. All of the changes across these domains interact with each other, as do environment and genetics, experiences and perspectives, and all sorts of other individual factors, all of which makes every adolescent experience unique. That said, this complex process can be simplified into three broad but fluid stages of development. And as our children grow up, we need to grow up our parenting in response, learning and relearning what, how and when to let go, or to hold on, or to embrace the next new thing for us both, and ultimately finding a healthy way to ride the emotional tides this inevitably brings.

Early adolescence (roughly 10–13 years): Puberty brings with it changes to bodies (which can make young adolescents very self-conscious), changes to hormones (which can make their moods both erratic and dramatic), changes to the wiring of their brains (which can make risk both more appealing and harder to manage), changes to the role their friends play in their lives (which can affect the decisions they make), and changes to their perceptions of their parents and caregivers (which can feel anything from unsettling to confusing or alarming on both sides). While some children will take much of this in their stride, for many others these changes will combine to bring big, new emotional experiences, and adults in the front line need to ready and steady with their own emotions as much as they can. This can be very hard when we may also be experiencing big, new emotions ourselves in response. One thing for certain, though, is that early adolescents need as much stability around them as possible.

Middle adolescence (roughly 14–17 years): Physical changes will mostly have finished for females, but for males these will continue for a while yet. Loyalty to their friends becomes fierce, while anxiety about the perceptions of their peers, and acceptance by their peer group, can profoundly affect their self-esteem, self-confidence and self-worth. During this stage teenagers will generally be exploring their sexuality, and for some their gender identity, while also experiencing their first romantic relationships, with the emotional highs and lows these can bring. The struggle for independence that started with puberty is still going strong, which often results in battles to gain ground, with all the frustrations (for teens) that being thwarted can bring and all the fears (for parents) that can come with letting go, and making those judgement calls about whether they can or can't cope safely with particular freedoms. Again, some will breeze their way through this, but for most there will continue to be lots of big emotions all round.

Late adolescence/early adulthood (roughly 18–24 years): By now, physical development is done, emotions are for the most part more stable and the desperate quest for separation from their caregivers that was all-important not so long ago will, for most young people, turn into a reconfigured adult relationship. The brain, however, has more work to do before it is fully grown up and as useful as it needs to be to help them through pressured or risky situations.

The busy adolescent brain

Adolescence is a time of enormous change in that pre-teen, teen and young adult head, transforming their brain from what they need it to do as a child to what they will need it to do as an adult – all of which takes around 15 years. It is a process akin to rewiring. The adolescent brain is a busy place, hard at work generating new neurons (brain cells that send and receive information) at a rate around four to five times faster than the adults around them, while at the same time pruning away those neurons they no longer need or use.

What lies behind some of the more typical teenage behaviours is down to the fact that this is not a smooth and even process. Racing ahead is the limbic system, the social, emotional centre of our brain, deep within which lies the amygdala, where our fight-or-flight response sits. It's also where we register pleasure and reward, and we know it is hypersensitive and super responsive in adolescence. Taking its time, and lagging behind somewhat, is the pre-frontal cortex, which doesn't fully develop until the early to mid-twenties. This is the crucial part of the brain that when mature will help them with planning, organizing and thinking things through to their possible consequences. It also helps regulate emotions, control impulses and manage that all-too-developed limbic system, but young adults can't fully rely on this until they reach their early to mid-twenties.

As adults we bring a balance of logic and emotions to our decisions, and sometimes one trumps the other in ways that don't always lead to the best outcomes. In adolescence, finding that balance, during this stage of unbalanced development in the brain, is hard. The limbic system is exceptionally sensitive and responsive in adolescence, so feelings will be experienced more profoundly and passionately than at any other time of life. Teens can encounter a very different degree of pleasure and reward from new and exciting experiences than adults, especially when those experiences involve taking a risk. If you are anything like me, the adrenaline thrill of a huge rollercoaster ride was as appealing as a teenager as it is appalling in my more mature years!

Teenage heads and hearts are also incredibly finely attuned to social and emotional variables. They can experience uniquely intensely both the pleasure and reward of feeling accepted by their peers and the devastation of being excluded where and when they feel it matters. That social risk-and-reward dynamic plays a significant role in adolescent decision making, just at a stage of life when the sensible pre-frontal cortex is least able to weigh in, press pause and take charge. However naturally cautious they are, research shows they will almost certainly be more likely to take a risk when they are with their friends than when they are on their own. Understanding all of this as a teenager is a huge step on the way to staying safe.

My day job, my life's work and mission now is supporting young people to make safer choices about drugs and to manage risk safely, and to equip the adults in their lives to help them to do this too. Much that lies around what is specific to drugs is entirely relevant to managing any and all of the risks teens will be exposed to, and there is a lot that parents and carers can do.

Managing risk and managing our response

About a year before he died, Dan and his classmates had been to Berlin on a school history trip, a definite highlight of his 16-year-long life. I have many photos from this time that his friends have generously shared, including one of Dan and two of these friends standing at the edge of a frozen pond, with snow all around and Dan's foot hovering over the icy surface. I have conjured up for myself a scenario that makes this a perfect picture of those different pulls of 'should I, shouldn't I?'. I have no idea if this was what was really going on, but knowing Dan, I can well imagine him thinking it looked like amazing fun to walk across the ice, see how far he could get, maybe skate around a bit in his boots and generally amuse the collected company. But knowing Dan, however tempted he was, he would also have been a bit cautious, conscious of the risks of the ice not holding his weight, falling in and getting cold and wet, and possibly worse. On his left is one friend – let's call her Amy – smiling and looking at Dan's hovering foot, and in my imagined scenario she is encouraging Dan to do it. 'It'll be so much fun, and if you don't try it, you'll never know. Just do it!' or words to this effect. On the other side is another friend – let's call him Connor. He has an arm round Dan's shoulder and a foot firmly braced against the metal edge to the pond. I imagine Connor urging Dan to be careful. 'Is the ice really strong enough? What if you fall through? Even if it's not deep, you'll be cold and wet with a long way back to base in freezing temperatures and that'll be pretty miserable.' What did Dan do?

Which of us doesn't have those voices in our head (or at our side) when we are making decisions? In our teens these voices can sound very loud and ring very true, sometimes leading us into harm's way. As parents and carers, we want to amplify the voice that helps them take a moment, weigh up risk, consider all the 'what would happen ifs' and navigate the situation safely. The voice of Connor, in short. We can do that by helping them regulate their emotions, but also by working with them when they are out of the emotional heat of those moments of decision making, to help them develop strategies that allow them to hear that sensible voice clearly through the limbic system clamour. One way to do this is by thinking through scenarios together and working out realistic, practical responses. If they found themselves in a particular situation, what might make it hard to manage safely? What could they do to help themselves through? What if that didn't work? What else might they try? While scenarios will change with ages and stages, doing this together can help them develop the skills needed to arrive at safer decisions when on their own and with their friends. The cool context of a conversation at home is, of course, very different from being with their friends, with all the social emotional stuff fully engaged, but it does help if they have 'practised' beforehand.

The challenges of the emotional context work both ways, for adult as for child. Calmly contemplating the theoretical risks of imagined scenarios doesn't test our own emotional regulation like the actual, real-life risks our teens may ask us to let them face. Parents and carers of teenagers inevitably find themselves having many a conversation about whether they can – or can't – be trusted to navigate safely whatever the next adventure might be, whether big or small. In these situations, managing our own emotional response can be tough when our parental/provider pre-frontal cortex is all too aware of the risks and possible consequences, and our natural inclination can be to panic. Taking a breath and pressing pause really can help in such moments, when we're presented with having to make a decision ourselves and our immediate instinct might be to lock all the doors and hold that teenager tight.

Our most important role is to grow our child into a happy, healthy, independent adult, and the measures we put in place to help them get there safely will naturally change dramatically over the years, from the tiny baby, helpless without our care, to the great big teenager increasingly stepping out into the big wide world without us. Our challenge is to make sure protections and boundaries are there that will enable them to stay safe, at a time when we are not always feeling entirely confident where that boundary now needs to lie, as they encounter experiences that are new to both them and us, and we have to weigh up their capacity to cope with the risks these might bring.

This all requires constant judgement calls, for which staying calm maintains best access to a clear-thinking head. A perfectly normal and natural teenage response to parental behaviour that stops their fun is to resent and resist any protections we put in place and to rail against, knock down or sneak around the boundaries put in place for their good. They can bring to this all the emotional intensity of a thwarted teenager. As parents we are standing in the way of the freedom for which they earnestly strive (though often, also, inwardly, sometimes secretly fear) and forcing them to face the social penalties of not doing whatever it is they want to do. However, despite all of this, boundaries are important and necessary and they need to know they are there, much as they might think they don't. It helps·keep them safe externally, but evidence also shows it builds internal resilience that will help them manage risks more safely by themselves.

This said, it is important and necessary to be flexible about where these might lie, at different stages and for different activities and with different social groups, because we do need to learn to let them go and to trust them to manage risk safely without us. Negotiation is key, explaining your rationale, listening to any objections, and remaining open to perhaps making concessions and agreeing appropriate safeguards if you do. Through all of this, keeping the focus ultimately on their safety helps, although keeping calm when emotions on both sides are running deep can be difficult.

Emotional regulation – theirs and ours

Teenage emotions can be unpredictable and disconcerting and can topple the equilibrium of the most emotionally regulated parents and caregivers on the front line, who love them more than life itself and want nothing more than for them to be happy. Our natural instinct, when faced with our child in pain, is to do all we can to take away the pain. However, maintaining positive mental health doesn't mean avoiding painful feelings – which, of course, can't be done in any case. In *The Emotional Lives of Teenagers*, psychologist Lisa Damour writes: 'Mental health is not about feeling good. Instead, it's about having the right feelings at the right time and being able to manage those feelings effectively.' There is so much that we as parents and providers can do to help them know what the right feelings at the right time look like and to help them develop the skills needed to manage these feelings in a healthy way. And the better we are able to do this for ourselves, the better a position we will be in to help them manage theirs.

We know that big emotions can be more alarming for adolescents than they are for us. But if they see us manage the difficult emotions we encounter, we then model how to do this to them. We can also model how to best respond on those occasions when we don't manage our own emotions well (which will happen – we are only human) by pausing, breathing deeply and finding our feet before moving through difficult emotions from a stronger, better internal space. Sometimes, however, we will need help too, whether from a good book (like this one!), a good friend who can help us offload, or a professional who can help us address any underlying issues. In essence, caring for our own emotional wellbeing is essential for helping us to care for those of our teen better.

Talking and (really) listening

Simply talking issues through really does help, as many studies have shown – and it's not just the process of translating a feeling into a word, sentence or story, but also knowing that someone else knows and cares. Simply telling you about something that's going on for them is likely to help make it feel better, however hard it might be for you to hear that your child is struggling or in pain. The key to this is connectedness with our teens and communication channels that are open enough, enough of the time, for you to be that safe place they can bring their difficult everyday stuff to. Connectedness and communication are very much interrelated and interdependent and one can and will strengthen the other. Connectedness can take many shapes and forms that will shift as teenagers grow, and as a parent or carer we will likely find ourselves needing to be more creative, responsive and opportunistic to strengthen that connectedness through these years of emotional turbulence. Key to communication with the teenagers in our lives is listening, something that is a lot harder to do well than many of us realize.

The first step to effective listening is by actually being present – an obvious point I know, but being available for that moment when our teens might need our ears is something that can take conscious effort, especially when our own lives and commitments are already stretched. When our children are small, we have to be with them continually, but as they get older they can seem to need (and want) us less. But in reality they need us just as much, if not more. They just need us differently and that includes needing to know we are there, whether in person or at the other end of a message or call. So the first step is being there and the next step is really being there by being present, focused and attentive. We know teens can often pick the most inauspicious moments. We might be in the middle of something we can't break off from easily (in which case promise to come and find them when you can, making sure to keep your promise, always). We might be exhausted at the end of the day – some teens take the tail end of the day to get around to finding a parent to unburden to. We might have our heads full of the stresses of work, or be preoccupied with wider worries, or just planning tomorrow's shopping list. And how easy is it to be distracted by notifications pinging through on our phones? However, breaking off and being present, and really listening, is one of the greatest gifts we can give.

Here's what I have learned

Giving teenagers our full, focused attention can be reinforced through our body language, encouraging responses, nods of the head and so on (and most importantly by putting our phones to one side). Try not to interrupt, tempting though it can be. Letting them get to the end of whatever it is they are offloading shows that what they are saying has value and interest to you (while also preventing you from cutting them short before they get to the most important part!) Showing empathy is important, even if you think their feelings are misplaced or even when you disagree with what they are saying. Acknowledging their feelings validates them and sometimes this can be enough in itself. They often don't want us to fix it, or them, or at least not right now – just as we often want someone to hear us out about how rubbish our day has been and not to come up with solutions about how we can make tomorrow better.

Verbalizing back what they have said and double-checking that this is what they were actually saying buys you some time to digest and process while also helping them to hear back what they have said from the 'outside' – and also showing that you've been paying attention. Developing your skills in posing thoughtful, curious, compassionate questions (something that can take practice) is helpful for prompting and encouraging your teen to talk, as well as helping you and them explore these conversations more widely and deeply. Helping them extend and improve their emotional vocabulary and fluency enables them to better name their feelings and describe them more precisely in a way that communicates more. Never feel you need to rush to respond. Take those deep breaths or step away if you need to in order to process what they have shared and to bring your own emotions into check. You may also need to take a pause during the conversation. Often we find that we stop listening (despite getting off to a good start) because our mind and emotions have spiralled into a tailspin of panic, getting lost in the worst-case scenario, or we are busy composing our wise response and working out how to fix it. Take time out if you need to, but let them know you'll be back, and don't leave them too long wondering.

We know many teens find talking very difficult. While there are many reasons for this, often it's a delicate balance between creating opportunities to talk and not putting them on the spot, or pressuring them if they don't want to talk to you or don't really know how to articulate what is going on anyway. Maximize those less confrontational and more comfortable, side-by-side situations – like sitting in the car, walking the dog, washing up. Keep your radar on high alert for those non-verbal messages that can hint at a specific emotional state, through body language, behaviour, interactions with siblings, and so on, although it can take very sensitive eyes and ears to spot the signs. Ask those curious questions. Perhaps suggest they talk to another trusted adult (or a professional) if you can see they are becoming weighed down with a burden they won't, or can't, let you try to lift.

One of the phrases I continue to bear in mind during difficult moments is the 'good enough' parent, coined by paediatrician and psychoanalyst D. W. Winnicott around 70 years ago. As someone with 'could do better' riven through every vein, this has been wonderfully reassuring. According to Winnicott, as long as an infant felt safe and loved, they could both cope with and forgive the shortcomings of their caregivers, and that counts for teenagers too. We will never get it all right, and during those teenage years we can sometimes feel as though we get it all wrong (though we honestly don't!), but every time we do, we have the chance to make amends.

Remember, even if it really wasn't down to us and we are still feeling battered and bruised by the experience, the ball always starts in our court because we are the grown-ups. It's up to us to pick up the pieces and go back to our teen to let them know that they are safe, and loved, and always will be, however that translates itself into the needs of a particular moment. We know there's absolutely nothing they could do that would make even the tiniest dent in our love for them, but it never, ever hurts to remind them and this in itself can help, and heal, all by itself.

What I wish my younger self had known all those years ago is that the most critical voice was the one in my head – my peers, it turned out, had a much higher opinion of me than I ever imagined they did. I know I didn't get it all right with Dan, but despite all I got wrong he remained a bright, bouncy, funny, kind and compassionate boy, from toddler to teen, growing into a fine young man, able to tolerate his parents' many flaws with great good humour. He was a boy who, among many other things, took a drug which took his life, but he was also a boy who knew he was loved. Who was himself infinitely, enduringly lovable. There's a lot I wish I'd known, but I did know how to love him with all my heart. I just didn't know how to keep him safe. And that's what I'm doing my best to fix for others. I hope this helps you.

4

Bridging the gap: using the African ethic of relatedness to unite generations

Dr Judy Blaine

'The world interacts with itself. The sky, the spirits, the earth, the physical world, the living, and the deceased all act, interact, and react in consort. One works on the other and one part cannot exist nor be explained without the other.'

Yusufu Turaki, *The Trinity of Sin*

Note to reader: For the past decade, first working in schools and more recently as an academic researching adolescent wellbeing, what has struck me most is a real sense of disconnection in our world: disconnection from ourselves, from others and from our environment. Western ideologies of individualism, competition and consumerism have led us to believe that we are separate from one another, and it seems that the further we go along this path of disconnect, the more evident the sadness and despair becomes.

With this in mind I reflect on my childhood and the strong sense of relatedness and interconnectedness that I learned from the Xhosa people and my gratitude for the profound impact this rich culture has had on my life. It is my hope that I am able to pass this wisdom on to my children and others so that this can be reflected in their own lives too.

Growing up as a white girl on a farm in the Eastern Cape of South Africa during the apartheid era inevitably shaped who I am today. Straddling two cultures, my British ancestry and the Xhosa culture into which I was immersed, influenced me in ways that I would come to appreciate only later in life. My siblings and I were all given Xhosa names; mine was Nomhle, meaning 'Mother of Beauty'. Reflecting on this, perhaps it was known then that I would indeed be mother to four beautiful children, who were born and raised in yet another culture – that of Hong Kong.

As an infant I was mostly wrapped in a blanket or towel on my nanny Nonzwakazi's back, *ndandi belekwa*. Being the youngest of four children, I spent a lot of time with Nonzwakazi and her family, who lived and worked on the farm. It was here that I learned the Indigenous conceptions of *Ukama*: relatedness and interconnectivity, that our wellbeing is inextricably bound with all that exists and that it is through this connection that we give and receive love. This interconnectedness allows us to share our lives, share ourselves and share the planet. Nonzwakazi taught me about our essential interconnectedness with nature, about the plants and animals used in traditional medicines and the myriad customs and rituals called on to appease the ancestors.

Although not my mother tongue, *isiXhosa* was probably the first language in which I became fluent. While my parents spoke to my siblings and me in English, it was listening to *iintsomi* (fables) around the fire, playing 'jacks' or stick fighting with my playmates, Polathi, Mzwandile and Thembile (children of the farm workers who also lived on the land), that I became fluent in *isiXhosa*.

I also recall spending many happy hours in the big truck with my adopted uncle, Ntuku, picking up injured animals on the farm, collecting feed for the cattle or taking animals to the abattoir. We would always pack some *padkos* (snacks), usually naartjies and biltong, for these trips as we innocently laughed the hours away.

By learning the language of the Xhosa people, I inevitably gained an insight into their rich culture too. From Ntuku, I learned the importance of the ancestors, who act as intermediaries between the living and spiritual realms and God. Ntuku would explain how dreams played an important role in divination and helped us better connect with our ancestors, and how really paying attention to our dreams could be helpful in solving all the problems I would face in my life. I learned the importance of honouring ancestors to bring good fortune.

And it was here that I learned the African ethic of *Ukama*, although I did not become acquainted with the actual term until a few years ago. Derived from the Shona word, *Ukama* encapsulates the idea of interconnectedness to past and future generations, of what it means to be a person in relation to other humans and the more-than-human world.[1]

This sense of interconnectedness is echoed in many Indigenous cultures and religions. Identity, in the Māori culture, is based upon *whakapapa*, a set of relationships with the living and the departed, the individual and their environment. *Whakapapa* suggests that everything in the natural world shares a common ancestry. Similarly, *Mitákuye Oyás'iŋ* (a phrase from the Native American Lakota language) reflects the worldview of interconnectedness. The phrase (roughly) translates into English as 'we are all related'. Interconnectedness is also relevant in religions like Buddhism which claim that the boundaries between self and others and self and environment are blurred or non-existent. Likewise, the basic ideal of Hinduism is that we are all interconnected, and that we are all made of the same stuff, *atman*.

As a five-year-old I went to boarding school to be 'educated', a privilege not granted to my Black friends on the farm. There I learned about our colonial past, the investments made in infrastructure and trade, medical and technological advancements, and how seemingly superior this empirical science-based knowledge was over traditional knowledge. The sad truth, however, is that, for most of my childhood, I was oblivious to the social issues that were facing my country, and indeed the world, and was unaware of the connection between colonialism and capitalism and ignorant of social and environmental crises. While I partly attribute this naivety to my young age, this concept was supported by the colonial prescriptions of what was taught in our schools.

This was a far cry from what I learned from Ntuku and Nonzwakazi, who believed that we were all connected, no matter how much our egoic minds try to tell us otherwise, and that anything we do impacts others; in other words, the choices we make today affect us, our families, our communities and future generations. That it takes a village to raise a child and that this interconnectedness gives all of our lives meaning; it gives us love and allows us the opportunity and security to help us flourish – echoed by Archbishop Desmond Tutu, head of the post-apartheid Truth and Reconciliation Commission: 'We think of ourselves far too frequently as just individuals, separated from one another, whereas you are connected and what you do affects the whole world. When you do well, it spreads out; it is for the whole of humanity.[2]

It is time to embrace this timeless concept so we can realize that our wellbeing is inextricably bound with all that exists. For the sake of clarity, I am adopting the acronym **Ukama – Ubuntu, Kinship, Accountability, Morals & values, and Alliance** – to help us all and future generations unite and live happier and more meaningful lives.

Ubuntu

The Xhosa people have a strong oral tradition with many stories of ancestral heroes and traditional customs passed down between generations. As infants and young children, my siblings and I spent a lot of time with our Xhosa childminders and their children. All four of us had our respective nanny whose sole responsibility (or so it seemed to us at the time) was to entertain us. This they did, always, regaling us with stories and *iintsomi* from their culture. It was from these kind, open-hearted people that we learned the meaning of *Ubuntu*, of kindness, interdependence and solidarity. One *iintsomi* I remember in particular was the story of the lion and the mouse:

> One day, the lion caught a mouse and was about to eat it. The mouse begged for his life, promising the lion that he would one day repay the lion's kindness by helping him. Soon afterwards, the lion was trapped in a net set by hunters. The tiny mouse heard the lion in distress and quickly chewed away at the net, setting the lion free.

As a young child I learned that kindness is significant above all else – it is the glue that bonds us together.

The concept of *Ubuntu* is derived from the Zulu proverb 'umuntu ngumuntu ngabantu', which roughly translates as 'I am because we are' The idea is beautifully illustrated in the Zulu greeting *sawubona* (literally translated: 'I see you'). But *sawubona* is more than a polite greeting as it also says: 'I respect you, I value you, you are important to me.' In other words, it recognizes the worth and dignity of the person being greeted.

Grammatically, *sawubona* is plural, meaning 'we see you', as in the Zulu tradition, like most African cultures, 'we' is used rather than 'I' to reflect the umbilical connection we all have with our ancestors, who are always with us. So, when I meet and greet you, it is not only myself that is doing so but also my ancestors whom I represent.

Ubuntu is the belief in a universal bond of sharing that connects all humanity; a worldview that emphasizes the interconnections and interdependence of self with others. The emphasis is on the collective spirit, the value of community and of caring and sharing with others. *Ubuntu* acknowledges our responsibility to other fellow humans and to the world around us. Once we acknowledge this common humanity and interconnectedness, the 'I' and 'me' will automatically become more 'we' and 'us' – a thinking that is easy to forget in linear, individualistic societies. As fellow *Un:Stuck* contributor Mindahi Bastida writes: 'We have to go from the I to the We. From the Me to the We. It is the time. And that is the reason we are here.'

Thankfully, we are starting to see deeper exploration of the importance of this sense of interconnectedness in the fields of psychotherapy and mental health. In his book *Intraconnected*, Dan Siegel coined the phrase 'Mwe' (Me + We) as the integration of self, identity and belonging.[3] In doing so, he redefines the concept of self as one of being intraconnected with all others and all that is. Similarly, in *Attuned*, spiritual teacher and author Thomas Hübl writes: 'It may take only a small number of us to establish a new level of collective coherence – to share our light, heal our wounds, and realize the unawakened potential of our world.[4] This is the essence of *Ubuntu*.

Ubuntu highlights the power of the collective and of standing together for the common good, such as the #MeToo and #BlackLivesMatter campaigns that both shared a powerful message that we, our global family, stand united. *Ubuntu* teaches us that we are not alone and that together we can be a force for change, for a better world.

Ubuntu also encourages us to see ourselves in others so that our own experiences can be kinder, richer and more connected. If we look at others and see ourselves reflected back, we will undoubtedly treat them with more compassion and kindness. This is *Ubuntu* and it recognizes the inner worth of every human being – starting with ourselves. Nelson Mandela imbued the true essence of *Ubuntu*, leading South Africa through a peaceful post-apartheid transition.

In her book *Everyday Ubuntu: Living better together, the African way*, Mungi Ngomane, granddaughter of Archbishop Desmond Tutu, shares advice to help readers bring the basic principles of *Ubuntu* into their own lives. This advice includes:

- See yourself in other people.
- Strength lies in unity.
- Put yourself in the shoes of others.
- Choose to see the wider perspective.
- Have dignity and respect for yourself and others.
- Believe in the good of everyone.

- Choose hope over optimism.
- Seek out ways to connect.
- Understand the power of forgiveness.
- Embrace diversity.
- Acknowledge reality.
- Find humour in our humanity.
- Know that little things make a big difference.
- Learn to listen so that you can hear.

Kinship

Kinship is the relationship between people with shared attitudes, a common origin and living a common life. Ntuku explained to me that, for the Xhosa people, kinship is one of the most vital forces in their lives. The *iziduko* (clan names) are as important to their identity as their names and surnames. On meeting, it is considered polite to enquire after someone's clan, a courtesy that is deemed to be the highest form of respect.

Kinship is also a system that has outlined family responsibilities, boundaries, interactions and rights. Yet again, the maxim 'It takes a village to raise a child' comes to the fore, suggesting that raising a child is a shared responsibility of the biological parents and the kinship formed by extended family members and close others that is beautifully portrayed in the Zulu tradition. When someone in the tribe behaves inappropriately, instead of punishing them, they are taken into the centre of the village, surrounded by the entire community, who remind this person of their qualities and all the good things they have done. When this happens, all present repeat *sawubona*, which in this context means 'I see all of you, your experiences, your passions, your pain, your strengths and weaknesses and your future and you are valuable to me'. The person then responds with *shikoba*, which means 'So, I am good, I exist for you'. The purpose of these meetings is to remind the person of their importance within the community and guide them back towards the path of good. These words are so powerful – they are so much more than greetings, they remind people that they are loved and valued.

We are hardwired to connect with others. It's what gives purpose and meaning to our lives. We need to be reminded that we are seen, we are loved and we are valued. When we feel that we belong and are not alone, we are better able to manage stress and cope more effectively with difficult times in our lives. To quote researcher Brené Brown: 'A sense of social connection is one of our fundamental human needs. Connection is the energy that exists between people when they feel seen, heard, and valued; when they can give and receive without judgment; and when they derive sustenance and strength from the relationship.'[5]

Our wellbeing is inextricably linked to our childhood, which in turn is influenced by the lives of our parents and ancestors, and we carry a huge responsibility for what grievances and trauma, blame and shame we pass on to our children. Numerous studies have shown how intergenerational trauma can be expressed as unexplained anxiety, fears, phobias and depression, while books including Mark Wolynn's *It Didn't Start with You*,[6] Resmaa Menakem's *My Grandmother's Hands*[7] and Thomas Hübl's *Healing Collective Trauma*[8] help us realize how our children and grandchildren are shaped by more than their genes and how by being a good ancestor we can enhance the wellbeing of future generations as well as our own.

Many of us tend to think of ancestors as those who have gone before us, but ancestors exist in a continuum of time, of generations, in the past and in the future. One generation builds on the next and in essence we are the ancestors of the future. And ancestors are not only those people to whom we are biologically related; they are any person whose past life has shaped our own life. Our descendants own the future, and the decisions and actions we make now will impact generations to come, so we need to be accountable.

Accountability

The words of French playwright and actor Molière (1622–1673), 'It is not only what we do, but also what we do not do, for which we are accountable', have long resonated with me, most especially in terms of my own accountability for climate crisis, social and economic inequality, racism and racial inequality. Although many of us are sensitive to these (and other) social issues, is this matched by a willingness to take personal responsibility and to actually do something about them?

Accountability refers to an obligation or willingness to accept responsibility for one's actions. When a person accepts responsibility, that person is committed to generating positive results, what some would call 'taking ownership'. In fact, accountability is an unexpected but powerful tool for motivation, and to me, a prerequisite for change.

Naturally, there are aspects of our ancestry that we take pride in and certain other parts that shame us. For those of us whose ancestors have been the cause of pain and suffering, we need to acknowledge our share of responsibility, express remorse and make good again. As a white girl growing up in apartheid South Africa, I undoubtedly assumed a privileged social position. And when I say privilege, I do not necessarily mean wealth. I am referring to the rights and advantages that I, as a white South African, got to enjoy. For far too many years, I was oblivious to my unfair advantage, oblivious to the inequalities that existed, and I did not think to hold myself accountable for the overt and covert racism of my country. I took for granted my access to education and other resources.

A few years ago I read a speech given by deputy principal Kevin Leathem to pupils at a school in Johannesburg, South Africa.[9] 'Dear white pupils,' he said, 'you're privileged. Do something about it!' Leathem tells us to acknowledge our privilege and do something meaningful with it. It is only when we recognize that we are part of the problem that we can also be part of the solution. For me, it has taken time, and continues to do so, to truly accept accountability for my social position. To quote American author and professor Adam Grant: 'It takes curiosity to learn. It takes courage to unlearn. Learning requires the humility to admit what you don't know today. Unlearning requires the integrity to admit that you were wrong yesterday. Learning is how you evolve. Unlearning is how you keep up as the world evolves.'[10] Each one of us is accountable to learn and unlearn, for ourselves, our children and future generations.

We also need to be accountable for our own health, physical and mental, so we can better support that of our children. Asking my young adult daughter for her insights into the mental wellbeing of her generation, she commented that most of her friends wished that their parents had gone to therapy, so that they don't have to themselves!

Every parent wants to do their job responsibly, generously and maturely. In her book titled *The Book You Wish Your Parents Had Read*

(*And Your Children Will Be Glad That You Did*) psychotherapist Philippa Perry shares her ideas on how to be a better parent.[11] She invites us to examine our own childhoods, to find the painful areas, to delve deeper and explore our own reactions to our children's behaviour. She reminds us that 'we are but a link in a chain stretching back through millennia and forwards until who knows when. The good news is that you can learn to reshape your link, and this will improve the life of your children, and their children, and you can start now.'

Without asking us, today's younger generation is challenging us to look in the mirror and address our own mental wellbeing. Young people need us to be honest with everyone, including ourselves, and we need to understand how our own upbringing continues to affect our parenting. We must know our limits, establish boundaries and not be afraid to apologize. We need to accept that we make mistakes and will continue to do so and be open to change and to rectifying our oversights. I know that many of us were not taught to do this, as our parents believed it was not their duty or obligation to apologize to their children. But we owe it to them and this we must do.

If we explore the concept of *Ukama*, we can see that this is potentially the ultimate form of accountability – an understanding and recognition of interconnectedness, where everyone cares about and looks out for one another and the environment in which they live. Accountability starts with us. Each one of us is socially, morally and legally accountable to the community or organization to which we belong. Once we frame accountability through the lens of integrity, we acknowledge and realign our actions with our morals and values.

Morals and values

Although my parents were raised as Christians, and as children my siblings and I were exposed to Bible stories often with powerful moral messages, it was the many hours spent sitting cosily around the Aga listening to the timeless *iintsomi* set in the wildness of the vast African landscape that truly captured my attention. In these stories the animals were given human attributes as they talked and sang while demonstrating human characteristics, always underpinned by a moral lesson.

I was the youngest of four children, so 'The King of the Birds' was particularly relevant to me and has remained with me ever since. In this story the birds of the forest gathered to elect a king. After much discussion, it was decided that the bird that could fly the highest would be chosen as king. The goose flew for a full day, the eagle for two and the vulture kept flying for three days directly towards the sun. Thinking he had won, he yelled in delight, 'I am highest, I am king.' But then the small voice of a sparrow could be heard: 'Actually no, I am the highest, I am king.' The sparrow had held on to the great wings of the vulture as he flew upwards into the sky. The vulture tried to shake the sparrow off his wings without success and gave up. Returning to the forest, the birds were amazed at the sparrow's feat. The tiny bird was declared king of the birds. The moral of this beautiful story being that leadership is less about size and more about skill and wisdom. You may not feel as skilful or successful as those around you, but if you play to your strengths and use your creativity, you can be victorious.

My own four children were born and raised as expatriates in Hong Kong. Bringing up my children in a multicultural society and with an expatriate lifestyle far removed from my own came with its own challenges. Trying to instil my own values and expectations in them, when many of their friends' families had different ideas, proved quite difficult at times. I needed to continually evaluate my core values, assessing which came more naturally to me and which felt misaligned or inauthentic, and why. I found using fables and metaphors very useful for instilling values in my children. Stories that focus on moral and ethical complexities encourage children to discuss and reflect on situations requiring an ethical response. Most evenings we would choose particular stories aligned with our value system from treasured books like *African Fireside Tales* or *When Hippo was Hairy* – stories of jealousy, pride, laziness, lying and stealing. Some of these stories helped instil values like honesty, courage and integrity in my children, just as they did for me growing up. As the children got older, I would use current affairs or movies to reflect on the presence or absence of ethics and values as a way of setting the moral compass.

We know that children learn best from adult role models. While this has worked well in past generations, today's youth receive mixed messages about the merits of having morals and ethical principles. In the digital age we are seeing a generation shaped more by their peers and social media than in previous generations. In their book *Hold On to*

Your Kids, Dr Gordon Neufeld and Dr Gabor Maté suggest that modern culture and society do not actively support children's attachment to their parents and, as a result, many children today are becoming peer-oriented. In their opinion peers are effectively replacing parents in shaping children's identity, values and moral codes.[12] And not always in a good way. And so, as parents and teachers, in addition to finding ways of 'reattaching' to our children, it is important that our positive messages, our morals and integrity are stronger and more convincing than the conflicting messages they are bombarded with on social media. To do this we need to understand what our core values really are and how we can be the best role models for our children. It is these core values that provide the moral compass for us and for our children.

Alliance

We often hear older generations (born 1946–64) dismissively describing Millennials (born 1981–97) and Gen Zs (born 1997–2012) as 'snowflakes', believing them to be lazy, entitled, overly sensitive or too 'woke'. Conversely, Gen Zs and Millennials are angry at and often intolerant of older generations, blaming them for ruining the world, often using the meme 'OK boomer' to dismiss or mock the attitudes of Baby Boomers for their apparent denial of climate change, resistance to technological developments, and opposition to the values of the younger generation. While this topic is worthy of a book in itself, it is important to acknowledge this difference in values and opinions between older and younger generations.

We must be careful that, while describing the collective attributes of a particular generation, we do not exaggerate the differences between generations. While there are clear generational differences in attitudes and viewpoints, there is much common ground and an acknowledgement that we all learn from one another.

From youth activists to religious leaders, we are hearing the call for an alliance between generations, to bridge the gap between them. Pope Francis spoke of this in July 2023: 'We need a new alliance between the young and the elder, so that the lymph of those who have a long experience of life behind them can irrigate the shoots of hope of those who are growing up.'[13]

In this age of disconnect we need to unite generations. Our world needs both the experience and knowledge of our ancestors, traditional and Indigenous knowledge, and the energy and social mindedness of today's youth. So much so that this interdependence and interconnection of generations is essential for the survival of our communities and our world. Coming together in our collective wisdom will help us and our world, and as the older adults in this equation, we must take the lead by creating environments in which our children feel valued, loved, seen and heard. When we bring young people into our conversations, they will remind us of our role as ancestors and they will carry our stories and wisdom to future generations.

What I wish I had known when I was a young adult

I wish I had known that all of life is interrelated. Whatever affects one of us directly affects all of us indirectly. Everything we do in life is laying down cultural and ecological tracks that will define the lives of our children and future generations. I continue to remind my children that how we navigate this world matters. How we speak, act and behave towards others matters. It really matters. And through many years of research and experience, words don't get more powerful than these by Nelson Mandela: 'Sometimes it falls upon a generation to be great. You be that generation.'[14] This is our calling. It starts with us.

Nuturing interrelatedness for living a more meaningful and interconnected life

- Appreciate that you are a mere link in the great chain of life, not the chain itself.
- Work on your trauma, insecurities and issues.
- Treat your elders with respect.
- Seek out and listen to the voices of the future.
- Be a custodian of the Earth and a steward of the future.
- Share accountability for the future.
- Learn to become better story bearers and filters, confront injustice, and find ways to forgive and be forgiven.

Notes

1. Grange, Lesley Le, 'Ubuntu, Ukama and the healing of nature, self and society', *Educational Philosophy and Theory*, 44:2 (2012), 56–67.
2. Ngomane, Mungi, *Everyday Ubuntu: Living better together, the African way*. Harper Design, 2020.
3. Siegel, Daniel, *Intraconnected*. W.W. Norton & Company, Inc, 2023.
4. Hübl, Thomas, *Attuned*. Sounds True, 2023.
5. Brown, Brené, *The Gifts of Imperfection*. Hazelden Publishing, 2022.
6. Wolynn, Mark, *It Didn't Start with You*. Penguin, 2016.
7. Menakem, Resmaa, *My Grandmother's Hands*. Central Recovery Press, 2017.
8. Hübl, Thomas, *Healing Collective Trauma*. Sounds True, 2020.
9. Lindeque, Brent, Speech about white privilege (2018). Retrieved from https://www.goodthingsguy.com/opinion/white-privilege-jeppe-high-speech/
10. Grant, Adam, Post on Twitter (now X), 2021. Retrieved from https://twitter.com/AdamMGrant/status/1437408114899357699?lang=en
11. Perry, Philippa, *The Book You Wish Your Parents Had Read (and Your Children Will be Glad That You Did)*. Penguin Life, 2020.
12. Neufeld, Gordon and Maté, Gabor, *Hold On to Your Kids*. Ballantine Books, 2006.
13. Pope Francis calls for a generational alliance of youth and elders, July 2023. Retrieved from https://www.plenglish.com/news/2023/07/23/pope-francis-calls-for-a-generational-alliance-of-youth-and-elders/
14. https://www.nelsonmandela.org/

5

Learning in the age of distraction

Dr Karl Sebire

'We are drowning in information but starved for knowledge.'

John Naisbitt[1]

I have worked with teenagers since I was one myself, first as a tennis coach, then in various roles in education, from boarding school master and classroom teacher to my current role in educational research. Through the years *Urban Dictionary* has been my secret weapon for keeping pace with the ever-changing lexicon of the teenager. When I had to decipher what the acronym TLDR signified, the fact it meant 'too long, didn't read' summed up my decade's worth of research.

I spent 11 years acting *in loco parentis*, at boarding schools both in the UK and Australia. Although they might not have been my own children, if you can picture what it's like to manage 60 adolescent boys at bedtime and the fight to get them all to put away their laptops and phones – it was a challenge. When not in the boarding house, I was in the classroom. There is no greater environment for witnessing first-hand how teenagers' attention spans are shifting, where the already demanding role of the teacher to be interesting now becomes one where the window to grab the focus of their audience is smaller and smaller. Beyond this, the past decade has been dedicated to trying to understand how learning has (or hasn't) shifted to adapt to an audience whose needs and media diet are unlike those of any other generation before them. Through my research, I've come up with a few possible answers.

Technology continues to advance at a rate which provides people with greater processing power at significantly more accessible costs. This constant connectivity presents both opportunities and risks that are at once exciting, multifaceted and unpredictable. With the ever-increasing saturation of technology in daily life, the impact on education continues to be significant, with augmented and virtual reality, artificial intelligence (AI) and large language models, game-based learning, advancements in 3D printing, cloud computing, increasingly affordable software and hardware, and cheaper devices all contributing to the rich suite of resources that educators now have access to. The passing of time will also witness a change in generations of teachers, with younger educators having a better understanding and appreciation of the digitally native lifestyle.

Our digital diet

The reliance on technology to work is paramount in civilized societies. It facilitates transactions, security, businesses, telecommunications, travel, infrastructure and societal needs, all of which are highly dependent on systems that are working constantly in the background. We become cognisant of these invisible technologies only when there is a fault, breach or failure in their functioning. Security breaches and system crashes send communities into crisis mode, and it is moments like these that remind us how dependent we have become on technology to function. This forced dependence brings with it a real sense of fear about what our increasing appetite for being online is doing to us socially, psychologically and neurologically.

One of the biggest cognitive threats is to our attention spans. With devices in our pockets, on our desks and embedded into our homes, from our TVs to our speakers, the call for our attention from a cacophony of interruptions has never been so loud. As author Johann Hari aptly puts it, 'Focus is not lost, it's stolen.' Ironically, it took many months for me to finish his *New York Times* bestseller *Stolen Focus: Why You Can't Pay Attention*.

Focus is a skill that is widely underestimated and reading a book places a high demand on our attention span. You may find that, unless your device is on 'Do Not Disturb' or powered 'off', then making your way through a respectable number of pages in one sitting can prove quite the challenge. Just turning the phone to vibrate is akin to having a mosquito bite but telling yourself you are not going to scratch it. And once you have finished reading, note how long it takes to revert to your mobile phone before starting to feel anxious. How much do you really think you have missed in the past 20–30 minutes? How about when the end credits roll at the cinema or when you are sitting at a red light or have 15 seconds to spare in an elevator? Consider your own technology diet for a few moments and how you might be able to help your mind uncover a little rest.

Is it any more virtuous a use of the screen when an adult checks the sport updates than their child playing *Fortnite*, or the adult attending to emails while the child is messaging on Instagram?

Focus is fast becoming the most valuable metacognitive currency in this age of distraction. Marc Prensky and others have labelled this generation the 'digital natives', as they have grown up in a world where technology has been embedded in their lives from their moment of birth.[2] We have conversations that vanish on Snapchat, news contained in 280 characters on X (formerly Twitter), and Instagram images that we scroll through with less than a second afforded to viewing each carefully curated, filtered image. Our brains are wired for instant gratification, satiating a need for the next hit of dopamine to our frontal lobe before we move on to the next video.

With the advancement of technology, our ability to maintain concentration on singular streams of information has been hindered, so much so that for many young people, and indeed their parents, being constantly connected has become the new normal. While multi-tasking is a term synonymous with technology use, academics warn that dividing one's attention between multiple operations only dilutes the efficiency, and often the effectiveness, of the process. Sometimes we forget that, while technology has advanced at an exponential rate, our biological make-up has not. Our brain has a limited capacity of functioning memory to attend to tasks, and technology can create the traffic jam that psychologists refer to as the 'central bottleneck theory'.

So how can we address this before becoming victims to the perils of life online? We must acknowledge that our brain only has a certain capacity for information and tasks at any one time. As soon as the brain becomes overloaded (which happens when we attempt multiple activities concurrently), the efficacy across each task is diminished. While monotasking is indeed a strength, when it comes to unrehearsed behaviours, being aware of when we are working efficiently, and when we are not, is the first step to controlling the distractions we are presented with.

An online world, but not by choice

The beginning of 2020 was much like any other. Hovering between white noise and discernible dialogue on the news in the background, something was happening across the seas in China that, in the early stage of January 2020, was an abstract and intangible concept to which the vast majority gave little thought in the belief that it would not directly impact their own small worlds. Until it did...

As the impact of a global pandemic landed on everyone's doorstep, so too did an entirely new scale of psychic numbing. Books, podcasts, empirical research, and psychosocial and psychological analysis will continue to interrogate both the short- and long-term implications of the Covid pandemic for years to come.

As a teacher, the pandemic taught me a lot about both myself and my students. As schools were forced, almost overnight, to integrate technological change that would otherwise have taken years to implement, we learned that, when thrown in the deep end, educators needed to swim. For those who have pursued this profession because they felt energized by engaging young minds, the ability to connect with students during this time meant far more than just opening one's laptop.

For me, one key takeaway from the overall experience is that being in the same physical space as someone else (especially my own students) is preferable, as the natural cadence of conversation can be stymied by a relay of accidental interruptions, as the micro-lag over video chat means people tend to speak in unison. Further, body language from the shoulders up can hide telling non-verbal cues, and both tone and intent can be lost through tinny laptop speakers. When there are more than two people in an online meeting or class, cross-talk is all but eliminated due to the confines of the medium.

Through these long months of virtual school, maintaining order in the online classroom was a delicate tightrope on which to balance. That said, all of the joy was not lost. We know that school is not just about absorbing content – it is richly coloured by the interactions, the fun and those micro-interactions of queuing up at the drink fountain, sharing equipment at lunchtime, or the adventures taken travelling to and from school. As the novelty of turning up to school from the bedroom swiftly wore off, motivation dwindled on both sides of the screen and the essence of what it meant to be 'at school' was reduced to pixelated thumbnails and emojis of acknowledgement. This said, I believe that the benefits of a hybrid model and finding a balance between online learning and physical attendance will eventually emerge as the new normal.

As a social scientist I have been able to reflect on how this seismic shift in society affected learning and our relationship with technology and what the longer-lasting implications may be.

For children across the world, education morphed into a variety of delivery methods. As a caveat, this perspective sits predominantly within a first-world lens, and both perspective and cultural sensitivity are key when looking at any aspect of what a Western lens would widely regard as ubiquitous access. Digital inequality has been well documented, and the divide between those with access and those without was starkly highlighted during the pandemic years. Recent studies have found that, for some countries, education ostensibly ground to a halt as students were kept apart from both their peers and teachers. Across parts of Central America, Africa and Asia, many students had to rely on education via television and radio broadcasts,[3] while, for some, even this was a luxury. In some developing countries, including Afghanistan, Bangladesh and Nepal, gender inequality also impacted access to online learning.[4] Added household responsibilities for female students, as well as societal contexts, imposed further barriers to learning. It is pertinent to remain cognisant of these contrasting contexts and to bear in mind that those with access to a device, reliable internet and teachers delivering content were the lucky ones.

The pandemic experience highlighted the fact that technology is a tool to supplement the many things we will achieve throughout our day. In the classroom, technology has expanded access to education and increased opportunities for communication and collaboration, while also giving students more ownership and control over their learning. However, none of these benefits are relevant if they are not guided by the principles of scholarship, empathy and understanding, which cannot be instilled by simply accessing one's device.

One of the core skills which schools must develop is divergent thinking – and this is where creativity becomes key. As we face a future in which artificial intelligence will replace many automated processes that once relied on human input, it is the creatives among us who will be able to devise solutions to questions that have not yet been asked. Regardless of the role academia will play in a child's future, the ability to take a blank page and turn it into a tangible concept is, and always will be, invaluable. As an educator, technology is one of the many tools we use to engage and to connect students with a broader world of knowledge. Technology will enhance the information that is available to teachers and students alike, yet its successful conversion from information to knowledge always depends on each individual's motivation to learn.

That said, technology is not a replacement for teachers themselves. If you are still paying your electricity bill at the post office in notes and coins, or walking into a local travel agent to book a flight, you may be one of the very few who have managed to curate a life off-grid. For the majority of us, asserting that we are going to live a life offline is harder than it may seem. And for young people, the line between online and offline is now so blurred that the concept of not having access to the internet is tantamount to having no electricity.

We have all learned that, when human interaction in its most basic form was stripped away, technology became the key conduit for connection, facilitating our ability to learn, to connect and to share. But for the adolescent, with a sponge-like brain still in development, how is it possible for them to discern signal from noise and take the abundance of information available and convert it into knowledge? Finding that critical balance is key.

Anxious parents – anxious children

One of the outcomes of this unique time in our history when children of all ages were under direct parental supervision (or close to) for most of their waking hours was a widely reported rise in parental anxiety.[5] This shared crisis, or collective grief, has led to a new set of post-pandemic parenting challenges. Since children were 'released' back into the world, many of them having missed out on key developmental stages, we are now witnessing schools and universities with a cohort of students having a very different appetite for risk and resilience. For many children, social skills and the ability to interact and collaborate with peers were stunted due to pivotal learning moments being removed from the classroom and siloed to the child's bedroom or kitchen. And for many of these young people, relearning what it means to be part of a collective can amplify anxiety, especially among those who have taken longer to readjust to school life.

Heightened parental anxiety is understandable considering the added concerns during these years with remote learning, economic uncertainty, health issues, social isolation and changes in parenting roles, among others, all without warning. A 2020 study by Yale University in the USA found that one of the most effective ways to address this childhood anxiety was by treating the parents, highlighting how a less anxious parent makes for a far less anxious child.[6]

This said, as life returned to the classroom, with a cacophony of laughter being the soundtrack to the school day, we should be buoyed with hope that the resilience it took to make it to the other side will ensure that this generation is prepared to flourish and thrive.

'Golden age' fallacy

We are all guilty of passing judgement in our observations of others, whether it be of the teenager who spends too long with their video games or the couple having dinner while glued to their phones. As an undergraduate studying design, I often teamed up with a deaf peer for group tasks. While neglected by others due to the communication barrier, I knew he was the best designer in our cohort and wanted to learn with him and from him. We often carried out our work in cafés, and to others looking on it appeared that we were constantly glued to our devices, yet this was our chosen communication channel. And it worked. We need to view technology use from a judgement-free perspective, acknowledging that human behaviour and human needs will vary wildly from one person to the next.

One may falsely assume that being a digital native provides us with the skills required to help us operate in this new world that are far superior to those of people who have come before us. In fact, research has shown that, while children may be adept at accessing games and entertainment, when it comes to utilizing the internet and their devices for learning their skills can be significantly limited because the intrinsic motivation that comes from seeking out entertainment is far higher than the motivation for seeking information for educational purposes.

With almost universal internet access introduced to them at a very young age, today's digital natives differ significantly from previous generations who have grown up with the smartphone and the tablet. With this comes a significant divide in opinion, with older generations tempted to focus on the 'golden age' fallacy – an over-romanticized notion that the 'good old days' were the best – and starting sentences with, 'Well, when I was young' as a lead-in to an argument about the downfall of the younger generation. We are all guilty of this as we think about how quaint it would be to live in a simpler time. But the sooner we acknowledge that the 'golden age' is now (whenever your now may be), the sooner focus can be directed towards the future and not on how our previous behaviours should frame current understandings.

Practical advice for maintaining a healthy digital diet

Self-regulation strategies can prove instrumental in finding that critical balance between harnessing the powers of technology while also ensuring that the deleterious impacts are minimized. While it is easy to focus on a task we are motivated to concentrate on, it would be naive to assume that everything we do is going to be as stimulating as watching our favourite movie or spending time exploring social media. In essence, being cognisant of our use is the first step towards overall balance. Some practical suggestions include the following.

For parents, teachers and all adults

- **Maintain a digital sundown**: put devices away before bedtime to avoid scrolling. Social media is intentionally engineered to keep viewers' eyeballs engaged for as long as possible, stealing many hours of precious rest time. Many apps are bottomless, meaning no amount of scrolling will reach the end of content. Therefore, the responsibility lies with parents and providers to know when to put devices aside.

- **Be conscious of divided attention**: dual screening (engaging with more than one device concurrently), or lapses in concentration that previously didn't exist, can be attributed to a stream of content that constantly regenerates every time we look away. If this results in habitually reaching for the phone, you must first acknowledge this as a challenge and then seek ways to moderate it by silencing the phone when watching television or turning it off when in the company of others, thereby allowing you to be more present. While it was once believed that multitasking was a strength, it can actually be the opposite. Where it is most effective is when one is conducting rehearsed behaviours. Think about the last time you tried to find a parking spot in a crowded shopping centre and turned down your radio without even thinking. Finding the spot in unfamiliar territory is unrehearsed behaviour and inadvertently turning down the music frees up cognitive load to attend to the task at hand. While technology is set to become increasingly embedded in social dynamics, it will not necessarily enhance an individual's cognitive capacity or mental processing power. Information that needs to be processed for later recall still requires our full attention and traditional methods of teaching and learning are the best way to facilitate this.

- **Don't measure yourself by others online**: we have all fallen down a social media rabbit hole where before we know it we have scrolled back five years on a stranger's Instagram feed. Our online persona is exactly that: the aspect of our character that is presented to others. The carefully curated catalogue of the 'perfect life' is engineered for validation and to present to others that all is well on the other side of the glass and metal under your thumb. If you find yourself lamenting that your life is not as glamorous or your physique as aesthetic as others you are observing online, a healthy follower audit and removal can do wonders for mental health. In essence, cultivate a feed that enriches your day, not diminishes it.

- **Be present**: a study by Sherry Turkle from MIT in the USA found that even the mere act of having the phone face up (instead of down) on a table can decrease empathy between conversation partners.[7] If you are more preoccupied with getting the perfect shot of your brunch instead of enjoying it with your present company, then it is worth recognizing your priorities. For those who may be shy in larger social situations, the easy retreat is into the phone to convey the appearance of being busy. However, this can limit human interaction. While using a device to capture our surrounds is fine, enjoying the moment is far preferable.

For those caring for teens and young children

While the following advice may just as easily be applied to adult life, the challenge for those caring for young people is to ensure that their technology use is safe, responsible and balanced. Please also read Chapter 3, 'Minding our (and their) emotions'.

- **Lead by example**: adults enjoy different privileges, as they rightly should. However, if you hold expectations around device use (such as no phones at the table), checking your own work emails over dinner is no exception. In other words, model the behaviour you want to see.
  Screen-free times and locations can help, such as not allowing devices in the bedroom (especially with younger children) or ensuring home WiFi is turned off at a suitable hour for older children. We know that sleep deprivation can result in reduced academic performance, decreased mood, and numerous further implications for a growing child's physical and mental health.
- **Encourage offline activities**: some children may be naturally active or social; however, for those more inclined to seek comfort in technology, we must ensure that time off-screen is part of their daily routine. Equally, it is as important to not frame offline time as a punishment but as a positive, whether that activity is with you or not.
- **Enable open communication**: technology should not be used as a bargaining chip, whether this be to punish poor behaviour or reward good. The only context in which this may be appropriate is if the technology is the cause of the transgression. Bear in mind that, if a child does not feel comfortable expressing their concerns about challenges they are experiencing online, in the fear that their device will be taken away, they may remain quiet and become withdrawn. Where possible, keep those communication channels open and active.

- **Educate young people about online safety**: continue to enjoy open dialogue so that you can learn from your child and they from you. Parents are most comfortable when they can control as many variables as possible, thereby eliminating possible threats. The challenge with providing your child with a device is that it grants them access to a world beyond the scope of visible parenting. It is therefore imperative to have open conversations, clear boundaries and expectations, and an understanding of what responsible technology use really means. Ideally, this is a partnership between messaging from school, parents and child. Accept that your child's peers' parents may take a different approach that can be used as a rationale for why they should be allowed to do something.
- **Be proactive**: if technology use becomes problematic to the point that the child withdraws from normal social interaction or activity, or the device becomes a constant source of conflict within the home, seek expert advice.

Technology is here to stay and it is up to us to manage it effectively. We must always remember that it is the child who remains at the centre of education's purpose. They should be encouraged to develop an understanding of how to maximize the potential of technology in a time where the boundaries between online and offline activity have become increasingly blurred. This affirmative approach will instil confidence in parents, teachers and students themselves to ensure that technology holds its rightful place in the learning landscape.

Notes

1. Naisbitt, John, *Megatrends: Ten new directions transforming our lives*. Grand Central Publishing, 1984.
2. Prensky, Marc, 'Digital natives, digital immigrants', 2001, part 2: https://www.marcprensky.com/writing/Prensky%20-%20Digital%20Natives,%20Digital%20Immigrants%20-%20Part2.pdf
3. Ayanwale, Musa Adekunle, Adewuyi, Habeeb Omoponle and Afolabi, Olakunle Waheed, 'Learning through radio and television during COVID-19: Perspectives of K-12 stakeholders', *EUREKA: Social and Humanities*, 2023, 61–72.

4. Mathrani, Anuradha, Sarvesh, Tarushikha and Umer, R. 'Digital divide framework: Online learning in developing countries during the COVID-19 lockdown', *Globalisation, Societies and Education* 20:5 (2022), 625–40.

5. Ng, Catalina Sau Man and Ng, Sally Sui Ling, 'Impact of the COVID-19 pandemic on children's mental health: A systematic review', *Frontiers in Psychiatry* 13 (2022), n. pag.

6. Lebowitz, Eli R. 'Parent-based treatment as efficacious as cognitive-behavioral therapy for childhood anxiety: A randomized noninferiority study of supportive parenting for anxious childhood emotions', *Journal of the American Academy of Child & Adolescent Psychiatry* 39:3 (2020), 362–72.

7. Turkle, Sherry, *Reclaiming Conversation: The power of talk in a digital age.* Penguin, 2016.

6

Humanizing the classroom: lessons learned by a head of school

Mary Lyn Campbell

'Just as Michelangelo thought there was an angel locked inside every piece of marble, I think there is a brilliant child locked inside every student.'

Marva Collins[1]

I looked out across my classroom at a sea of someone else's babies, and I realized that someone felt about all those children the exact same way I felt about my son. I knew that if someone ever treated him as a test score or a category on a rubric, it would break my heart. So, my challenge to you is this: put those young people first, realize that their achievement will come. That there is no need to rush it. It will happen. Look them in the eyes and tell them they matter. Remind them they matter until they believe you. Smile at them. Ask them how they are doing – and mean it. Because chances are, you're the only teacher today who has.[2]

These words by teacher, mentor and author Lindsey Acton are the very reason I began my teaching journey almost 40 years ago. I wanted to be that teacher and for the past years I have tried to live up to being that educator, with poignant memories of connecting with specific students and adults in schools evermore in my soul.

For me, this revered trust that we as educators are lucky enough to hold is the privilege of our position. We get to build up each child's belief that they matter. Educational spaces are not simply schools or a business that provides a service. They are the breeding ground for qualities that humanize our children and provide the platform for the generational transfer of knowledge and wisdom. After all, education is a profoundly ethical activity aimed at sharing knowledge and aspiring to cultivate good judgement and wisdom. It therefore becomes the task of all within a school system to ensure this story is heard and told by as many others as possible.

Typically, a school would say that what matters most is their mission, their curricular programme, their assessment practices, the sports and arts programme, the pastoral care, the quality of their teachers, their community, their accreditation process and their academic results and university acceptance rate. But are these really the most important components? Are these the only true measure of what being a good school really means?

Schools are precious places. We receive children at a very young age and have the capacity to nurture their sense of self, or not. I would argue that we have a sacred trust and that our job as teachers is to ensure that each little human that arrives at our doors is invited to connect with their essence in a safe and nurturing environment – one that is committed to helping them thrive and flourish.

Every day a delicate dance plays out in the classroom. Even though a child has physically walked into the room and is sitting in front of the teacher, this doesn't automatically mean that they are connecting with what we share with them, or that we become privy to their minds or imaginations, or can touch their soul. It simply means that as teachers we have a physical body in the room. It is the responsibility of every teacher to create an environment in which differentiated learning can occur. And this is an incredible challenge.

From a more physical perspective, humanizing the classroom means deinstitutionalizing the school. If we don't have a school space that is comfortable – every day students go through the motions with lights glaring down on them, sitting in a cold, soulless environment with hard chairs – how can we expect them to soften into themselves? But when we introduce softer furnishings, physical variation, welcoming practices and more personalized greetings, we begin to break down the barriers to learning and forge a more real and human connection with them.

As educators, our calling is to open the doors to understanding in all students that enter the room so we can help each one of them become a fully enlightened human being.

The call to protect, to care

When I was 11 years old my father received a death threat from terrorists, which galvanized my family into fleeing from our expatriate home in South America. For me, everything seemed frightening, violent, confusing and uprooted from the familiar. Searching for meaning during this difficult time, I asked my father, 'Why?' Why him? Why us? Why now? I remember him speaking to me with his gentle, soft brown eyes, saying that sometimes, when people feel powerless, they take it out on others, sometimes even to the extent of taking another's life. He went on to say that it was our responsibility collectively to create the circumstances that would never push a person into thinking that the only way forward for them was to kill another precious human being.

The experience of facing men with guns, hiding from harm, losing people in the bloody mess of confrontations and repeatedly second-guessing who you could trust in the raw edge of flight was emotionally painful and had a lasting impact on me. If ever I hear gunshots, that internal vulnerability and helplessness come to the fore. Nevertheless, I am grateful for these memories as they have served me well, despite the trauma.

Over the course of time, I have come to forgive the aggressors. I have endlessly reflected on the circumstances that led them to feel they had the right to threaten me and those I loved. What happened all those years back gave me the strength and resilience to face many of my fears and to prioritize what was, and still is, important for me.

It was also the emotional springboard that helped me jump into action during a shooting in the school car park many years later. That day many of us were sitting in on a leadership meeting when we heard the shots. I recognized the sound and could sense the fear in the alarmed reactions of the children and staff. My instinct was to protect, but I soon realized that others were too immobilized to react and to help. On exiting my office, I saw the maintenance staff and schools' guards approach me, and with a few requests to cover certain doors and redirect frightened students, we managed to clear the area. They remained alert and acted professionally under the circumstances. This incident has also stayed with me and made me think more about those people I can truly trust to be there when needed and who will care for others at the most critical moments in life.

This call to protect and to care is our sacred trust. Even in the most dangerous of circumstances our children should feel we are there for them and will do anything to keep them safe. Growing up in a world where children feel safe because they know that the adults around them will fight to protect their best interests reflects a defining characteristic of our collective humanity. Even during the recent pandemic, it was those children and communities that felt most protected and cared for that fared best.

I return to many traumatic stages in my life as moments that consolidated my belief that we have the collective responsibility to deeply care for one another in our communities and that we hold this responsibility regardless of our socio-economic position in society. After all, we were born to care, and life makes sense only when we do.

While most of my professional life has been spent in private or affluent international schools, my deepest inspiration has come through my project work with socio-economically challenged schools in developing countries. I fondly remember visiting a state school in Patagonia. It barely had enough classrooms or resources to teach. But what it didn't have in terms of a typical school budget, it made up for in the creativity, sense of purpose and loving, caring relationships that permeated every tiny corner of that school. The maths class was held in the playground using basic resources like pebbles and stones to help children learn, to a backing track of laughter, movement and engagement. Lack of resources was never going to deter any of those teachers from helping their students. This particular visit taught me a lot, mostly that learning and caring can happen anywhere and that often the best education comes when we find the means to be kind to one other and to connect through mutual passions.

Looking back on my 30-plus years in educational leadership I know that, while my thinking has matured, I have remained firmly rooted in my mission to help support children and adults in schools to feel heard, valued and loved. Paraphrasing Philip Moore in his 2017 book *The Future of Children: Providing a love-based education for every child*, the driving intention within schools should be to ensure that, through supportive and positive relationships, students learn the value of doing the right thing, at the right time for the right reasons, and that developing a strong sense of curiosity, connection to nature, compassion and a culture of care is critical for every community to thrive.

Where it goes wrong

Unfortunately, not every developing trend in education has supported the idea of creating a culture of humanizing care in schools. As society has become more litigious, schools have been obliged to enforce all-encompassing and restrictive safeguarding and child-protection frameworks and policies. While there are valid reasons why these protective measures are now common practice, when taken to the extreme (as is often seen today) they have created colder and more sterile interactions between educators and children. For instance, teachers and staff in school settings are often prohibited from lifting a child after a fall in the playground, and they are unsure whether hugging a crying child or offering a lift home to a student in a staff member's car is viewed as acceptable. In our attempts to protect children, we have also eliminated those well-intentioned warm and fuzzy interactions that help young children in particular feel safe and loved.

Another major change in recent years has been the emphasis placed on standardized and achievement-based curriculum plans. While many school programmes start out with a more inquiry-based curriculum, as children progress into secondary school the programmes become more linear and content based, creating overwhelming, stressful and problematic learning environments.

Being a school head or leader today is more complex and challenging than ever before. Not only have expectations about what education must provide changed substantially, social cohesion has diminished, as have beliefs in religious and values-based frameworks. At the same time parental and societal expectations about what schools should educate for have increased beyond measure. And feeling the need to respond, schools have added even more content to subject-based courses, introducing courses in digital intelligence, AI, programming and coding, as well as life skills and social emotional competencies – all of this being added to an already overflowing student plate. Yet still many of us question why our students are feeling pressurized and overtly challenged.

Having worked and lived through such immense change in the education system, leading a school amid these disruptive forces has only strengthened my commitment to developing healthier ecosystems for learning by facilitating a more positive culture of learning and high expectations and an enhanced, more nurturing culture of care. One question I often ask myself and my colleagues is: are our high expectations of academic achievement creating positive cultures of learning?

For many of us working in education today, the main focus of what we do is directed towards academic rigour and achievement to the exclusion of almost all else. While well intentioned, the irony is that, if we don't first build a solid relationship of trust and care with students, we inadvertently discourage them from reaching their fullest potential.

In *At What Cost?: Defending adolescent development in fiercely competitive schools*, Dr David Gleason describes a potentially calamitous panorama for both private independent and international schools, referring to the multiple, contradictory and unrealistic demands that are imposed on schools to deliver a specific type of education. The fact that many of these schools are also extremely expensive augments the pressure to respond to the fragmented and often ludicrous expectations frequently imposed upon them.

In my many years as head of school I have seen this play out repeatedly. For example, some years back on an admission tour of a primary school, parents asked me if this school could guarantee their child's entry into Stanford University. I wished those parents realized that no one can ever guarantee the way forward for any child. There are no 'service guarantees' – as one parent requested. Each child is so uniquely themselves.

I often ask myself and my colleagues what has driven some parents to place such high stakes around the educational achievements of their children. Many in the sector describe the current situation as a higher education 'arms race' in which the increased competition for spaces in brand-name universities, and the erroneous notion that students are served best only by getting into a branded university, has created a rather unfortunate situation for young learners. As if this rite of passage were a hero's journey, we co-opt them throughout their entire upper secondary school experience to plough through an obstacle course with the sole aim of gathering credentials that just might serve them in their university application.

I have also found that parental insecurities about what is best for a child can exacerbate tension, in the belief that you are only a good parent if you push your child to exceptional academic achievement.

So much so that far too often it seems that a child's life has become commodified, instead of simply allowing them to follow their own path of inquiry and innate creativity, nurtured by their developing inner world.

Throughout their childhood and adolescence, children attempt to define their identities. They need time to explore the dimensions of who they are and who they want to become, without having the adults around them decide this for them. The idea that the school system (in response to parental and societal expectations) should dictate to young people who they have to be and what specific personal learning pathway they must follow, thereby denying their authentic voices, is worryingly unhealthy and unsustainable.

If we were to survey teachers, leadership teams, parents and even educational bodies such as the International Baccalaureate Organization (IBO), there would likely be a consensus that there are negative drawbacks to imposing our expectations on students at this developmental moment in their life. When we read about the decline in motivation among students, the increasing behavioural outbursts, their lack of confidence and self-worth, rising physical disorders, diminishing mental health and increasing incidents of suicidal ideation, we must pause and ask ourselves why this is happening. As it sits now, the current teaching model is unsustainable for several reasons, yet it does not seem possible to dismantle the educational framework we work within for fear that changing the structure will impact a student's chances of getting into university, bringing an onslaught of parental criticism that schools are not setting high enough standards for rigorous learning outcomes.

Cultivating better learning ecosystems

Certain educator circles are starting to focus more on heart-centred education, recognizing that fostering positive and intentional relationships with students and other adults in a school enhances learning outcomes. Many of us have always known this. The more comfortable a student feels with their teacher and other adults in the school, the more likely they are to be excited about what they are doing and to play, to inquire, to be curious, to make mistakes and to take risks.

As head of school, every school morning I stood out in the playground, be it in hefty downpours, heavy snow or bright sunshine, with a big smile on my face as I welcomed students, families and staff into school. Much as I would like to believe that other aspects of my role as a head of school will be fondly remembered, when I meet former students and parents today, they still comment on how this one small act made a very big difference to their school day. It showed them that I was genuinely happy to see them and that I sincerely cared about them.

What can schools today do to help cultivate a more nurturing culture? They can start by implementing some simple rituals to help foster a real sense of care. For example, the practice of including regular circle time at primary level and tutor meetings at secondary are becoming increasingly popular. Circle time is a short period each morning during which an entire class of students gather together seated in a circle, greet one another and listen to others talking about how they are feeling emotionally, before discussing their learning goals for the day. This exercise in orienting oneself helps define how children feel, setting them up for a growth-oriented learning experience.

As children develop, tutor time in secondary school also provides a space in time to find a sense of belonging and connection with peers and to talk about activities across the whole school. By simply allocating 20 minutes each day to bringing students together in small groups, they start to build a sense of both individual and group identity with their peers and a deeper, more personal connection than what generally happens in a larger school assembly. I have found that creating that intentional space and time every morning makes a notable difference in building relationships while also framing the day in a positive, constructive fashion.

When a school is focused on 'positive education' (a phrase coined by psychologist Martin Seligman, director of the Positive Psychology Center in Pennsylvania),[3] how these initiatives are structured also supports character cultivation, social emotional competencies and wellbeing. For instance, preventative mental health software such as Flourishing at School, among others, can further support the development of wellbeing literacy and enhance student self-awareness.[4]

In essence, providing students with a platform to build their emotional awareness and maturity, to monitor and develop their mental health resiliency in order to help them emerge with a strong sense of identity, is a critical touch point for society at large. So much so that a 2023 societal wellbeing report by BIGGAR Economics in the UK concluded that 'the single biggest predictor of adult wellbeing is their emotional health at age 16, and although mental and physical health are important, poor mental health explains more of the misery in society than any other factor'. The report went on to note that 'relationships and a strong sense of community are important as is the quality of the physical environment'.[5]

This said, emphasis on students and their sense of care and wellbeing is not possible without the adults in schools also being listened to and feeling cared for, and while there are undoubtedly many positive stories of compassionate support and thriving supportive communities, the number of worrying incidents that continue to occur is unacceptably high. Often, we forget that some of the most emotionally complex and demanding jobs in the workplace are held by teachers, yet their support networks and access to structured practices to enhance their mental wellbeing are severely lacking.

It seems blindingly obvious that when children feel safe and happy they have the optimal grounds to learn and mature. Yet why is it that several of our schools fail to recognize the need to create cultures of care that authentically support students and adults so they can feel more valued, heard and psychologically safe, while at the same time maximizing their potential? Sometimes our interactions in educational institutions are reduced to transactional exchanges in which the focus is far removed from the needs of the whole student. To me, a fundamental aspect missing today is the deep and loving care needed to help us all feel recognized, loved and able to flourish. Early in my head of school career, Andy Hargreaves, research professor at Boston College and one of my intellectual mentors at the time, commented mid-conversation, 'You know, Mary Lyn, the only two important goals we should strive for in education and educational leadership are to support the development of learning and caring in schools.' However simple this may sound, focusing on learning and caring can prove a real challenge when trying to bring it into practice.

Where does it start?

Human work

We have all read about the rising rates of anxiety, depression and self-harm in communities across the world (see Chapter 1, 'An age of anxiety', for more). While there are many reasons why this is occurring, a conversation I recall with an eight-year-old student stays with me. When I enquired about why he was ruminating over self-harm and suicidal ideation, carrying the weight of the world on his young shoulders, he spoke about the multiple challenges the world would have to overcome and about the resilience his parents had indicated that he would need to address and solve these issues. He also spoke of the hopelessness the adults in his life felt in the face of current realities about climate change, environmental damage, economic recession, war and conflict, and he had seen his parents and their friends navigate depression, burnout, stress and much more. He was being asked to get the best grades possible in school, to learn multiple languages and to attend extracurricular activities, almost daily, with the end goal being his university application, eight years later. He felt overwhelmed and incompetent, and at the age of eight was asking himself what was the point, and whether he might as well end it all now.

We sometimes forget that children really do listen to our conversations. Not only are they exposed to our attempts at dealing with often difficult issues, they are also privy to an increasingly polarized social media that paints the world in ways that are divisive, frightening and fragmented. We know that children (and adults) thrive when they feel safe and hopeful about an often-uncertain future. Nevertheless, many of our narratives at personal and societal levels can be overly pessimistic as they create stories that unintentionally can cause others to suffer.

In my opinion, reframing our exposure to negative and toxic narratives and being conscious of when we fall into or generate them ourselves is a first step towards change that will impact both our own wellbeing and that of others around us, most especially our children.

Yes, it takes a village to raise a child and schools depend on many stakeholders to support their mission. Through their narratives and actions everyone with a voice, from teachers and educational authorities to politicians and external third-party providers, can equally impact, positively or negatively, the wellbeing of the children in their collective care. And by being more mindful of the narratives we collectively use in front of children, and ensuring they are developmentally appropriate and not condescending or demeaning, we can ensure that students, including that vulnerable eight-year-old boy, do not become utterly overwhelmed by the world.

Another disturbing tension I have witnessed over the years is the mutual or one-sided disrespect between parents and school leadership and staff. On many occasions teachers are inclined to assume they know what serves the children in their care better than the parents do. Frequently I have heard learning specialists label a child with a specific learning difficulty or diagnosis without first considering the parent's emotional reaction to the assessment. I have also witnessed callous interactions between school leaders and parents or staff members suffering a family crisis, a loved one's death or job dismissal.

Yet again, I ask myself and my colleagues what it is about our education system that so adversely affects our capacity to respond in a more empathetic and humane manner. Maybe we have been conditioned to believe that some of these responses are to be expected? That they are normal and this is just the way we are and the way society is? Having observed exchanges like these too many times, I strongly encourage all of us to know that we can do better. I challenge us all to think about how we can further humanize our responses at both society and school levels and what we must first consider to make this happen.

Character education

In his book *Hidden Potential: The science of achieving greater things*, organizational psychologist and professor at the Wharton School, University of Pennsylvania, Adam Grant writes: 'Most experts believe it's a combination of high-quality teaching, intrinsic motivation fueling deeper learning, lower stress and test anxiety, improving focus and character skills developed early paying off over time.'

Using Finland as an example of a more worthy education system, he adds, 'Right now, what we know is that Finland is the best in the world at helping students progress without monopolizing their time, wreaking havoc on their lives, or making them hate school. Their deepest underlying assumption may be that the tradeoff between doing well and being well is a false choice.'

Many schools underestimate the importance of incorporating a character education programme into their overall curriculum. In 2013 the UK's University of Birmingham first published the Jubilee Centre 'Framework for Character Education in Schools', calling on educators to provide an environment that supports students in building character.[6] The framework outlines the building blocks of character education, referring to intellectual, moral, civic and performance virtues that through 'practical wisdom and integrative virtue developed through experience and critical reflection enable us to perceive, know, desire and act with good sense'.

The Jubilee Centre's research identified that students gather character virtues as 'taught, caught and sought'. The framework encourages schools to reinforce these virtues in every space, activity, interaction and communication across the school's human ecosystem. In the microcosm of some school environments we see evidence of applied opportunities and activities that have been adapted from this framework and used intentionally, meaningfully and as a reflective part of whole-school practice.

In my experience, a useful self-reflection for schools is to assess how they intentionally teach for positive character traits, such as being respectful, responsible and kind, and how coherent their messaging really is. Also worth reflecting on is how teachers and staff in general actually model these behavioural virtues themselves and what they use to motivate students and other adults to strengthen their own characters. To this end the Jubilee Centre has developed a comprehensive audit of schools' practices to support character development.

Another question worth deliberating is to what extent schools actually follow Martin Seligman's positive education model. Numerous studies have confirmed that both using positive education interventions and nurturing character strength-based programmes in schools heighten life satisfaction and wellbeing in students.

To complete the questions, educators should ask themselves the following: What do we know about learning? What do we know about happiness? What do we know about human development and evolution? What allows us to nourish the virtues of a noble character?

What do we know about environments that support authentic student learning and development? How do we foster cultures of optimism and hope in schools? And what humanizes all of us within a school environment?

Answering these questions for myself, what I do know is that children who hold strong, loving, authentic relationships with a core group of people are more likely to develop grit, perseverance, curiosity and optimism – qualities that we know are essential to flourishing and thriving.

Reflecting on my years in educational leadership I know that it takes many adults advocating, supporting and caring for a child to ensure that they grow into happy, successful, responsible and capable young people. Each child is so uniquely themselves. For me, David Gleason's 2016 TED Talk succinctly sums up what all of us adults who support and care for young people must do:

> Our adolescents and our students rely on us not only to educate them but to take care of them. We owe it to adolescents everywhere to educate them and parent them in healthy and balanced ways, in ways that respect their development, in ways that do not hurry them or risk hurting them. For our kids' sake we need to acknowledge our collective responsibility in this regard, and then parent and educate adolescents accordingly.[7]

What I have learned

While for some, the task ahead for education might seem arduous, I consider much of it to be quite simple. Here is what I now know matters most.

Stories matter

When children learn words, they discover a way to speak that best represents their reality. Often, however, they use particular words to share the storylines of what they see and what they feel and know, but their words may be insufficient and do not adequately reflect what is really going on inside their minds. What is inside all our minds is unique to each one of us. Teachers and staff in schools must be sensitive to this so they can better tease out the stories playing out on the inside of every child.

The storylines we use in life become critical. As teachers we hear these 'stories' directly from children once they feel comfortable and safe enough to speak openly. In early years settings, stories come naturally for children, as they find their place, be it playing the hero they dream of becoming and the dragons they will slay, with relative ease and enjoyment. As children grow through their school years these storylines mature and if they are given positive reinforcement, they will use these stories to help them better define their unique identity in the world.

I often reflect on a former student who hero worshipped his father. He told me that he was nothing like his father – a mathematical genius who had built a career around his fluid understanding of mathematical literacy. The father told his son that learning maths was easy and that he just had to try harder. But every time his son was in maths class he blanked and was unable to assimilate the teachings or exercises. We assigned a tutor to support him. Being in Switzerland, this teacher took the young student skiing, watching him excel, all the while reminding him how brilliant he was at calculating the best angles to ski down the slope and praising his decisiveness at making the right decisions at the right moment. Slowly the young boy's confidence grew and he was able to transfer what he knew intuitively through action on the slopes to his understanding of theoretical maths, slowly changing the narrative of his story.

Each child learns differently and many need to make an association with something deeper and more tangible to better understand what is being taught. That's what these stories provide. They are our stories. We create them for ourselves driven by our need to make sense of things, and the more positive they are, the more we can use them and translate them into actions that serve our best interests.

In many ways, the narratives we generate for ourselves and those we take on from others influence our growth, our self-confidence and our self-determination. They offer a holistic approach that encapsulates the whole person, the fiction and non-fiction, and the emotion, while also allowing space for the undefined.

Receiving positive affirmations from others makes a difference to how we feel about ourselves. The words we choose to use have an impact on ourselves as much as on others, and embracing our own stories helps establish a solid platform for a happy and satisfying life.

Deeply embedded in each of our stories is the plot line – the very purpose and reason why we are travelling towards our end goal or destination. Helping children tap into their individual stories should be an essential aspect of every child's school day, and just maybe the advent of AI, if used effectively, offers a means to making this possible.

Curiosity matters

Every child is born with a healthy dose of curiosity. Letting them explore, inquire, wonder, play and pursue their own interests and dreams is key to developing their creative mindset.

In his 2016 TED Talk 'Do schools kill creativity?', the late Sir Ken Robinson said, 'Creativity now is as important in education as literacy, and we should treat it with the same status.' He recited a story about a six-year-old girl in a drawing lesson: 'She was at the back, drawing, and the teacher said this girl hardly ever paid attention, and in this drawing lesson, she did. The teacher was fascinated. She went over to her, and she said, "What are you drawing?" And the girl said, "I'm drawing a picture of God." And the teacher said, "But nobody knows what God looks like." And the girl said, "They will, in a minute."'[8]

How often do we hear this in the classroom?

Being told to stop daydreaming, to focus more and to ignore what is sparking their interest is killing every child's unique spirit. Finding a way to connect this inherent spirit with what they need to learn in the classroom, and giving them the space to allow their imagination to breathe, is mandatory for the ongoing growth and maturity of the whole person.

I recall one particular student who was frequently sent to my office due to his 'bad' behaviour. At times, he lived under my desk! Much of this behaviour was the outcome of his expansive, inquiring mind. He continually asked rather unusual questions, wanting to know how much pressure had to be exerted on a yogurt container before it exploded, for example, and how long he could stand on one leg while balancing a cup of water on his head. This young boy was trying to figure out the nature of force and gravity. But his teachers focused only on the consequences of what in their view were 'poor' behavioural choices. As I began to understand the patterns behind his behaviour, I encouraged him to experiment more. He did and later qualified as an engineer. It turns out that curiosity was the magic fairy dust for the current CEO of a large aeronautical multinational company.

In a world facing myriad issues, I often question why we continue to constrain our students within specific parameters. Why do we separate our disciplines? In my view, students should not have to choose between the straitjacket of academic expectations and narrow areas of study and curricular content at the expense of their innate creativity and interests. It should not be an either/or choice. For instance, students offered medicine as a career path should also be able to study philosophy, as understanding the ethical deliberations underpinning philosophy is hugely relevant to the study of medicine.

Creativity is a gift. We must use it wisely. But yet again, our linear, results-focused system is suppressing many of the gifts we were born to bring to life. To paraphrase Sir Ken Robinson, we need to see our creative capacities for the richness they provide and see our children for the hope that they are, by educating their whole being, so they can face this future. We may not see this future, but they will. And our job is to help them make something of it by not dimming these bright lights of curiosity during their formative school years.

Relationships matter

In my experience, when a student doesn't feel accompanied, when they don't feel heard or safe, then no learning can occur. The student's relationship with the teacher has to be appreciative, the teacher's relationship with the student's parents has to be cooperative, and the relationships established between teachers themselves have to be collegial. This solid fabric of mutual respect and understanding is the most successful platform any child can thrive upon.

Feeling that we are heard and valued is empowering. That connection to the other, that budding friendship or feeling of being cared for is such a vital part of every child's growth and maturity, helping them feel safe and confident enough to explore their potential. What better place than school to learn the basics of socializing, making friends and generating a sense of belonging?

In her book *The Dance of Connection: How to talk to someone when you're mad, hurt, scared, frustrated, insulted, betrayed, or desperate*, psychologist and relationship expert Harriet Lerner writes:

We must remember that our conversations and musings invent us. Students use their voice to build their identity. During their childhoods they need that space to form who they perceive they are and what adjustments they want to make to try to become the person they want to be. How we use our voice determines the quality of our relationships, who we are in the world and what the world can be and might become. Clearly, a lot is at stake here.

Kindness matters

If we choose to live only in the confines of our own reality and interests, our world quickly becomes an unhappy and soulless place. Kindness is a selfless act towards others that contributes to the wellbeing of us all and it is fundamental to ethical maturity. To be kind is to cement the foundational elements of a civilization in which people work together and support one another, so that collectively we can reach our highest selves.

We often talk about how selfish others are, but maybe we need to think a little more about how often we thank others for the kind words or gestures they extend to us. Some years back a young student from a socio-economically wealthy family visited India as part of a school service project. On his return he wrote to me, saying, 'I can't understand how they can love so much, with so little.' With these words this young student understood the real meaning of kindness – something so beautiful to behold in the human spirit.

Think about the following questions for a few moments before answering: Do you act kindly to those around you? Are you kind to yourself? Do you act with empathy and compassion when others are suffering or are in a crisis? Do you ever engage in random acts of kindness? Do you help in creating a culture of care? Do you shine a light on the selfless care shown by others?

What does it mean to be a human being?

In my view, what it really means to be a human being has been simplified and reduced to sporadic Insta moments, where children are educated to get good grades in particular subject areas or to make a successful university application. But if we really think about this question, there is a great divide between the aspirational intent of education and what we currently use as metrics of success in the classroom.

In our complex, rapidly changing world we must prepare children for situations that none of us could have anticipated and we must help them to redefine what it means to be a human being within their own historical context. If they have the emotional awareness and maturity, a social fabric on which to fall back on when needed, and a real understanding of their own essence and spirit, what part of the future will they not then be prepared for?

The sacred trust of educators is to ensure that children are prepared and that they are well rounded, happy, responsible, capable and ready to do the right things at the right time and for the right reasons.

To connect with what we can fully be as human beings is an enormous task, and it takes a society, a community and informed parents to come together so the child can flourish and thrive.

Notes

1. Collins, Marva, *Ordinary Children, Extraordinary Teachers*. Hampton Roads, 1992.
2. https://www.teachingchannel.com/k12-hub/blog/heart-centered-classroom-management/
3. https://ppc.sas.upenn.edu/sites/default/files/posedseligmanadler.pdf
4. https://www.flourishingatschool.com/
5. https://biggareconomics.co.uk/wellbeing-indicators-across-the-uk
6. https://uobschool.org.uk/wp-content/uploads/2017/08/Framework-for-Character-Education-2017-Jubilee-Centre.pdf
7. https://www.youtube.com/watch?app=desktop&v=cSiE5iE0QMs&feature=youtu.be
8. https://www.ted.com/talks/sir_ken_robinson_do_schools_kill_creativity/transcript?autoplay=true&muted=true

7

Humanizing the workplace: timely advice for the future of business

Galahad Clark

I'm a cobbler. I make shoes. With our world in flux, the question every trade/businessperson now needs to ask themselves, their colleagues and their wider business network is how they can contribute to the very real challenges we are facing and help reconnect people with nature in the twenty-first century.

We are all indigenous to Earth, but a lot of us find ourselves refugees from our land and from our human nature – in business and in life. While the following words shine a light on my business, Vivobarefoot, I have written them simply to share what I have learned (often the hard way) in my many years developing our brand and embracing this journey of reconnection.

My hope is that my story will entice you to open your mind to a new, more natural and humanistic way of working and propel a more meaningful connection with your own existence, not only in the workplace but most of all as a human being. And while we are a long way off doing the perfect thing at Vivobarefoot, we are firmly aligned in working towards our vision for a more regenerative future for business, people and the planet.

A shoe story

The first footwear was made about 100,000 years ago. We humans don't have hooves or pads and needed to protect our sensitive feet from the hot, baked African savannah and the camel thorns as we learned to run down antelope through the sweltering midday sun. The prize prey was the eland, the biggest antelope, with the thickest skin that was preferred for making the original running sandals.

As humans travelled up through the Rift Valley and populated the rest of the world, 'we' made different types of footwear from available animal skins: buffalo sandals in the Indian subcontinent, bison, elk and deer moccasins for the first peoples of Europe and the Americas, reindeer boots made by the Sámi people in the Arctic, and so on – all simple foot coverings appropriate to the local climate, made person by person and foot by foot, that allowed the foot to do its natural thing while keeping our feet firmly connected to the Earth.

As horsemanship was modernized during the last few hundred years, saddles and stirrups were introduced (especially in Europe), as was pointed (easy to put in the stirrup) and heeled (to stop the foot going through the stirrup) footwear. Heeled and pointy shoes soon became associated with high status and the posh 'Western' footwear of the last few hundred years has been deforming and weakening our naturally wide and flexible feet ever since – distinctly different from the natural (wide, thin and flexible) footwear that humans would have worn for the last 99,000 years or so. Furthermore, in the twentieth century, as new rubber, plastic and foam technologies were introduced and the sports shoe industry took off, even these new lightweight shoes, to this day, mimic pointy-heeled work shoes with raised, padded heels and pointy 'go-fast' shapes. The modern footwear technology and the booming orthotics industry we are now familiar with (heel cushioning, pronation control, arch support, etc.) were invented to tackle problems caused by the footwear itself. At best a shoe matrix of pain, or at worst a shoespiracy!

The footwear industry of today, much like other big businesses dazzled by technological patents, has proven to be devastating to both human and planetary health. Children's feet have been weakened and deformed by non-foot-shaped, stiff-heeled shoes, with the vast majority of middle-aged adults experiencing various forms of chronic pain in their feet, knees, hips and or/back, much of this being the result of the modern footwear industry and sedentary lifestyles. With 24 billion pairs of poorly designed, badly fitting shoes made out of virgin petroleum-based foams and plastics, and leathers tanned with carcinogenic heavy metals that generally all end up in landfill, this is a major problem. Not to forget the padding, heels and stiff materials used that literally disconnect us from the Earth – the source of grounding and connection essential for a healthier and better way of living. This padded, patented disconnection from nature seen in big shoe brands is analogous to what is happening in big agriculture, big energy and big pharma, among others.

In my view it is the responsibility of business and industry to reconnect us to our source of grounding, the Earth, and to 'walk us home'. It is ironic that 10,000 years ago our ancestors used local sustainable materials to make shoes that kept us connected to the Earth and enabled natural, pain-free movement because they had no choice... and now 10,000 years later, we again have no choice.

In his seminal book *Sustainability by Design*, Dr John R. Ehrenfeld, former director of the MIT Program on Technology, Business, and Environment, defined sustainability as all life being able to flourish on Earth, believing that the only excuse for filling up the world with more stuff is that said stuff should connect us to nature, make us feel more human and answer important environmental or ethical questions.[1]

So, when considering where you might like to work, it is essential to ensure that the company you are looking at holds nature at the top of the hierarchy – in other words, a company that is fundamentally and philosophically doing 'the right thing', rather than what most businesses do today, which is to do the wrong things 'righter' (i.e. making shoes that deform your feet and literally disconnect you from nature, but making them from 'less bad', more eco-friendly materials).

For a cobbler this means making footwear that allows your feet to do their natural thing, made from materials with truly circular solutions. By circular solutions we mean either made-from-nature-to-be-returned-to-nature (i.e., compostable within a certain time frame) or made from truly recycled polymers. It is relatively easy to make a biode-gradable shoe that can compost in nature, but more difficult to make a high-performing shoe (as we know them today) that can compost within 90 days in your garden. It is also relatively easy to make a shoe out of recycled materials, but currently 'recycled' means 'downcycled' materials that are still on a degenerative linear progression to landfill (e.g. like a plastic bottle that becomes a fleece, then becomes a shoe or a playground flooring...). Chemical recycling or being able to take existing plastics and return them to the same-grade polymer (e.g. a plastic bottle can be recycled into the same-grade plastic to become a water bottle again) is the real circular challenge and no shoe company has achieved this yet, ourselves included.

For businesses to start operating from these basic principles, an important starting point is to organize themselves into natural systems. At Vivobarefoot we have chosen to align with the regenerative business movement led by sustainability and leadership experts Giles Hutchins and Laura Storm, authors of *Regenerative Leadership*, who for the past few years have had a major impact on the Vivobarefoot ecosystem and the Vivo Way.[2]

Within this context we focus on our 'outer' and 'inner' business journeys. The outer journey refers to the products and services we offer, which for us means that we need to be more than merely a shoe company. With this in mind, we have made a conscious transition to become more of a natural health brand, building an education platform both on- and offline, while also encouraging people to go on multi-year transformational health journeys that allow time out to regain their sovereignty and to live their human nature.

Our inner journey is equally important, especially as too many employees are forced into mechanistic hierarchical thinking (or boss pleasing) that takes away agency from the individual rather than allowing them to genuinely contribute to the overall customer experience. We have worked tirelessly to define the 'Vivo Way', which is not unlike Brené Brown's advice to her young daughter navigating this new world: 'Strong back, soft front, wild heart' (see Introduction).

The Vivo Way is linked with natural movement:

- Upright posture – head above hips, above feet: in other words, a clear business structure (each part knows where the other is).
- Quick rhythm – high cadence of steps and an agile fail-fast mentality: we aim to create a fearless culture where people can try things and, if they don't work, quickly re-step and try again. This is the opposite of long, lumbering strides, which once you make them are more difficult to re-step, with increased risk of fall or injury in rough patches.
- A more relaxed way: we know that stress and tension get in the way of efficient elastic movement, so even when times are tough, we continue to dance through the storm and improve.
- Sensory feedback: it is most important for our business that we are in a constant state of candid and honest feedback loops.

Within this Vivo Way framework we emphasize creating an inner culture based on the following key areas:

- An adult-to-adult coaching and listening culture: in essence, simply treating people as adults by allowing them to bring their full selves to work and by really 'listening' to them. For this to be effective, it must be framed through the lens of Self – Team – System and employees must be supported and valued as they work to cultivate connection on all levels. This also means a culture that respects good people and is trusted, with minimal rules and open, transparent information.

- A transparent culture and communication network that extends to benefits, pay and reward, through a system such as an evolution council: in our case, this comprises an arrangement in which multiple levels of the organization set company pay and reward across the organization, with integrated impact reporting that ideally includes B Corp – an increasingly popular accreditation system that scores and awards status to businesses based on how they act in terms of social, health and environmental capital, rather than just financial. Ultimately, good people should be trusted with full transparency and rewarded in a collegiate manner based on both financial and non-financial metrics.

- Flexible hybrid working opportunities: companies continue to learn how to make hybrid working 'work', with a significant number of jobs now amenable to adaptable working conditions – with this in mind, seek out an employer who is engaged with making hybrid working 'work' in the long term.

- A culture of investing in learning and development that offers opportunities to evolve within the organization: learning and development are key to every self-actualized person, and choosing an organization that helps broaden life experience and skill set, while encouraging people to pursue their hobbies and passions and inspiring them to become true masters of their chosen field, is essential.

- A commitment to support every employee's wellbeing: all organizations should actively support mental, physical and social wellbeing – after all, this is critical for a healthy, happy workforce.

Some successful initiatives at Vivo Life include:

- mental health first aiders and a coaching network that encourages people to bring their whole selves to work
- a nine-pillar natural health platform that all teams actively engage with and which includes ergonomic work set up for both offices and the home and opportunities to enhance every employee's physical health with ongoing encouragement and monitoring when requested to help people meet their personal goals
- an active social wellbeing dynamic with high degrees of psychological trust that we have found to be essential to a positive and fearless culture
- avoiding 'impatient' capital: this is the scourge of most purpose-driven businesses in the modern world. The number of brilliant purpose-led brands and businesses that grow to circa £20–50 million before being diluted (or, in most cases, destroyed) by impatient venture capital or corporate takeovers is devastating. Always look for a company with 'patient' capital that allows the company to drive the business forward across natural, social and financial capital – rather than one that focuses solely on short-term shareholder returns
- an organization that recognizes natural rhythms, thereby avoiding stress and burnout. At Vivobarefoot we try to work with seasonal flows that recognize fallow 'winter' periods alongside periods of 'spring' growth, 'summer' flourishing and an 'autumnal' harvest of recognition (this seasonal rhythm can be both shorter and longer than 12 months), and that are aligned with the company's value system, which in this case includes Simplicity (honesty and transparency), Dance (continuous improvement, flow and agility) and Diversity (innovation and creativity)
- being part of an organization with clear values that clearly leads with these values at its core: a company that employs the right people, that creates an aligned stakeholder group (suppliers/vendors/customers, etc.) and that lives in a world of regenerative relationships rather than (as is too often the case) degenerative, short-term economic drivers that destroy relationships and consistency and ultimately undermine purpose-driven brands. In our world, outdoor clothing retailer Patagonia is seen as an anomaly rather than the basic standard for all businesses. And the fact that it is the one company in the world that has scaled (to $1 billion-plus) while remaining true

to purpose, and the one company that has remained independent of impatient institutional investment, is no coincidence. The world needs thousands more Patagonias to ultimately show that it is possible to scale a business while keeping nature at the top of the hierarchy

- make every big decision in nature!

For a detailed case study of Vivo's culture, see Giles Hutchins book *Leading by Nature: The Process of becoming a Regenerative Leader.*[3]

Notes

1. Ehrenfeld, John R. *Sustainability by Design: A subversive strategy for transforming our consumer culture.* Yale University Press, 2008.
2. Hutchins, Giles and Storm, Laura, *Regenerative Leadership: The DNA of life-affirming 21st century organizations.* Wordzworth Publishing, 2019.
3. GIles, Hutchins, *Leading by Nature: The Process of Becoming a Regenerative Leader,* Wordzworth Publishing, 2022.

8

The house of tomorrow

Ed Olver

'Your children are not your children.
They are the sons and daughters of life's longing for itself.
You may house their bodies but not their souls.
For their souls dwell in the house of tomorrow.'

Kahlil Gibran[1]

I loved my grandfather. I was in awe of his stories of derring-do. A decorated Battle of Britain Spitfire ace, he won the Distinguished Flying Cross, was incarcerated in Stalag Luft III POW camp (of *The Great Escape* fame) and was lauded by his prime minister, Winston Churchill, who said: 'Never in the field of human conflict has so much been owed by so many to so few.' Latterly, he was a colonial farmer who fought to defend his family in the Mau Mau insurgency in Kenya (1952–60). I grew up in the warm embrace of his experience and basking in the reflected glow of his reputation. I wanted to be just like him.

This is my story about becoming *Un:Stuck* from a conditioned perspective by finding a flourishing union with life and a professional career geared towards personal transformation and societal renaissance. I hope my perspective and what I share here may encourage others to step out of the perceived wisdom of a materialist paradigm and into the power of their own innate sovereignty.

When I was invited to contribute to *Un:Stuck*, it was initially suggested that I emphasize the positives because we all need some form of existential hope to inspire and energize young people today; it's the kinetic power of evolution, after all. But I know that my role is not to mollify others but to enthuse and empower them. We want the younger generation to realize that they are entirely the architects of their own realities – and that these realities are unlimited. We need them to wake up to what life is and what their role in it requires. This will not happen unless we talk openly, honestly and deeply about how life, both personally and professionally, really works.

Life is not a ladder to climb for a box-ticking career and the benefit of external validation and egoic appeasement. It is the greatest privilege to be embodied in this extraordinary experience we call life, and yet so many of us get bamboozled into trading it. For what?

The following words are a letter of LOVE to children growing up in a fragmented experience, a world without the psychological handrails that have stabilized almost every other age in human history. But this is not the love of Hollywood in all its garish, saccharine schmaltz – it is a real, honest LOVE for what is good, what is beautiful, what is true and what is deeply transformational. It is the LOVE that recognizes wholeness and the LOVE of a fiercely and courageously open heart that speaks with clarity, coherence and intention. It is the very same LOVE that our children need to reconnect with if they, and we, are to persevere and flourish, and the same LOVE that Pierre Teilhard de Chardin understood would one day guide humanity's destiny: 'Someday, after mastering the winds, the waves, the tides and gravity, we shall harness for God the energies of love, and then, for a second time in the history of the world, man will have discovered fire.'[2]

This LOVE letter is also an invitation to parents, teachers and others who provide loving support for young people – and indeed young people themselves – to be brave enough to leave their subjective realities behind and to feel more deeply into an open, more embodied and interconnected perspective, with the courage to surrender all they think they know to be true and open up to a relationship with life, both professionally and personally, that none of us could ever possibly fathom. Living as we are amid an epidemic of loneliness, a crisis of relationship, and the most shattering statistics on self-harm and suicide, is there an alternative?

I hope from reading these words that you will create your own reality, not as a product of what has come before you but by scaffolding the future you want for yourself and for others of your generation. This is not the future your ego desires but the future your soul needs to become *Un:Stuck* and to flourish.

Before we proceed, let me answer the question: 'Who am I?' I used to think that this question really meant 'What have I achieved?' until I discovered Ramana Maharshi. As the son of a corporate expatriate participating in the glamour of globalizing capital I was programmed for a conventional path from an early age. When I was 18 I landed on a trading floor in the naive belief that stewarding money was how to become whole. After university I went to Royal Millitary Academy, Sandhurst and then served in Iraq, interdicting the Iranian Quds Force delivering IEDs to the Jaish Al Mahdi in southern Iraq. Latterly in my army career I was adjutant of the Household Cavalry Mounted Regiment, initiating and executing a diplomatic engagement that was recognized by a crown prince as an event that 'consolidated the eternal bonds of friendship linking two sisterly nations'.

Following all of this, I built a commercial foreign policy company in 17 countries, became engaged to a Hollywood actress, and was embroiled with intelligence agencies and the people that pull the levers of power in a geopolitically strategized world.

When I reached the pinnacle of what I had long been told I 'should want' in my life, everything changed almost instantly. A succession of immensely challenging experiences led to a very deep sense of betrayal that permeated my whole being. While the pain was excruciating, I soon realized that these experiences were the mirror I so desperately needed and I knew then that the experience could not have been created by anyone else, other than myself. I was and am the architect of my reality. It was a simple and yet profound realization. I had not been betrayed; I had been betraying my true self. I recognized that I had completely misunderstood the purpose of existence. I was very successful at manifesting whatever I wanted, when I wanted, but I had never considered the reasons why, or really asked myself the question 'Who am I?' or indeed considered what the deepest part of me truly wanted in my life.

By living my life from the outside in, I had achieved everything I had put my mind to, both professionally and personally. Although my operating system was creatively sound, the source and intention of what I was achieving were not grounded in authentic connection. Instead, I had become a product of my experiences and had relinquished my focus and attention to conditioning and the prevailing culture. I did not know myself at all.

I also realized that I wasn't all those plaudits and baubles of self-congratulation, nor the expectations of others, but inside of me there lived a quiet voice that was deeply connected to my heart and that always spoke the truth.

I have no regrets about the path I walked as it seemed quite normal then, but as perspectives broaden, it becomes easier to see more clearly how we can serve more deeply. Since 2017 I have been focused on projects that can seed a renaissance of being. With so much fragmentation and polarization in the world, there is more opportunity now to be guided by one's internal compass. In this age we need not place our hearts in the hands of patriotism or national interest, as these are increasingly unsafe vessels. Service like humanity can and should be universal. Where once I went to Sandhurst because I wanted to 'Serve to Lead', now young people can unite across identity and serve something far greater with more purpose than ever before.

The bow and arrow of life

We will transcend this dark moment in history just as our ancestors have done, but to do so we need to hack into our internal operating systems, which in recent years have become fixed, corrupted and malignant. We need to be realistic and address the trauma and the taboo deep within us all.

As a culture we have become lost and dislocated from the truth of what it means to be human. We are junkies of our internal reward systems; our dopamine and adrenaline have been hijacked and co-opted by consumerism and social media toying with our fundamental need for wholeness and connection. We are sold stories of greater relatedness, but, in truth, the reverse is true. We are lonelier and more disconnected than ever before. The dominant forces of global capital and technocracy have all but extinguished the essence of what it means to be human, and the impact of the growing incremental changes on our collective psyche and wellbeing is already manifesting.

No, we are not okay, but realizing that everything has its equal and opposite and knowing that it is only by walking through the fire that we can begin to see the light of transformation, this moment represents a rare opportunity bestowed upon this generation. The anxiety many of us feel is the gift of awareness, and the sensitivity it invites is the signpost to change, and now it can be utilized to culture more aligned actions and outcomes. Universal principles seek homeostasis and harmony, and so by addressing our internal transformation we can then precipitate external change.

The renowned activist and peace campaigner Satish Kumar (see Foreword) reminds us that 'economy' semantically means 'the management of home', and so the definition of what we recognize our home to be and what we intend it to be is fundamental. So, we must ask ourselves: What is our true economy? And how can we metamorphosize this Attention Economy into a more human-centric Age of Awareness?

Psychiatrist and author Iain McGilchrist speaks of the need to 'string the bow', a timely and comforting analogy for what is needed today in the belief that we cannot fire the arrow forward into harmony unless we welcome the tension created by the polarity of the bow arms. As poet and mystic Kahlil Gibran wrote, 'You are the bows from which your children as living arrows are sent forth. The archer sees the mark upon the path of the infinite and he bends you with his might.'

Our role now is to hold this bow and arrow close and pull hard on that string so we can create the depth of draw that will allow us to witness not only the mark on the target but the journey there too. We need to create the critical force that transfers energy from the bow to unleash the arrow forward into a more harmonious future – a future where human beings are liberated back into their true nature, so they can enjoy a closer, more trusting relationship with their higher authority and realize that the real power resides within themselves, not with their employers, politicians or national narratives.

The rehumanizing reformation

Traditionally, humanity lived tethered to family, community and a commonality of societal norms and expectations that was proportionate to the reach of information available. But the advent of the World Wide Web in the 1990s, when information became radically transparent and ubiquitous, changed this dynamic for ever. While the impact was not immediate, we now know that it has dramatically altered the architecture of human organization.

ChatGPT, which to some has become the bleeding edge of the Information Age, defines humanity thus: 'Humanity typically refers to the collective attributes, behaviours and characteristics that define the human species. It encompasses qualities such as compassion, empathy, morality, and the capacity for intellectual and emotional growth.' But as every Indigenous community, spiritual insight or religion with thousands of years of wisdom recognizes, the non-dual, interconnected nature of everything makes this definition seem quite impoverished. The tools of our current dominant paradigm have somehow, in just 400 years or so, deleted relationship, spiritual growth and the evolution of our consciousness from this definition of humanity.

Currently, it is the dominant dogmatic narratives of corporate-funded globalist politicians enmeshed in a system of perpetual growth on a planet of finite resource that are the embodiment of power and control.

Contrary to this, the Achuar Nation, an Indigenous tribe living in the Amazon who only connected with the outside world in the 1990s, see many of our CEOs and political leaders as 'possums' – or someone who is still operating from their ego that has not yet crossed over into a way of being that recognizes a more unified relationship with life itself. For example, the Achuar use forest initiations as their 'rite of passage' for young people moving into adulthood, and they invite the use of psychedelic plants in jungle immersions to support the transformation of neural pathways from 'me to we'. They become one with the Forest and recognize the interdependence of life. To them, this is the sign of maturity and it is why they view our systems as adolescent.

But this narrative is starting to change as we are realizing just how ignorant the mantra 'Move fast and break things' really was. Humanity in our finely balanced ecology must be cautious when moving forward and not make decisions for short-term commercial gains, quarterly reporting and investor returns, without consideration for the ultimate environmental consequences of these actions. (See Chapter 7 for more.)

Intention is what turns a tool into a weapon and likewise with information technologies (IT); rather than seeing them as being dangerous, let us reframe the narrative by seeing them as an opportunity to enact the urgent change that is needed in the workplace – and in life at large.

As renowned inventor and businessman Thomas A. Edison said, 'There's a way to do it better – find it.' This is our mission, and I remain steadfast that the future of 'Work' (with a deliberate capital W) will ultimately be the complete antithesis to what it currently is and has been over the past generation or so. It is my belief that 'Work' will no longer be what we seek to achieve outside of ourselves. This 'Work' will be our inner engineering. No longer linear, we will come to recognize that our interplay with life is more interactive and multidimensional than we ever imagined possible. Everybody will recognize their own destiny as the source of their inspiration and their life's work will be to align their personality with their soul.

In truth, we are no different from a seed germinating or a bird flying in migration. We are living a perfectly coded expression of 'life meeting life'. And once we choose to accept that reality is much more than a linear series of stories imprinted into our impressionable minds, we can begin to make wiser decisions about how to live better and how to work in a more humane and compassionate way – a way that benefits all of life, not just the select few.

A most informative example of the possibilities of evolution is illustrated through sport. If one reviews the earliest recorded film clip of the men's high jump during the 1896 Olympics in Athens and then watches Javier Sotomayor clear 2.45 metres to set the world record in 2010, it is clear that we are the very same humans, just 114 years apart. What is fascinating, however, is how nutrition, training, technology, technique and perspective have transformed human capacity within a relatively short time period. The invitation now is to hold ourselves open for this pending rehumanizing reformation. If the Fosbury flop can revolutionize the high jump, why can't we have a radical reorientation of perspective and an awakening to our true nature and our life's purpose?

Work and life therefore need not be a struggle. It can, and should, become natural and in flow, a succession of interactive experiences guiding us to wholeness. While this requires some degree of faith, a flowing aligned energy is the dividend of this reciprocity, and the more one invests in giving, the more the investment grows and the more life itself will flourish.

Inside each of us lies the duality of the Soul versus Ego, Higher Self versus Conditioned Self, Heart versus Head, and our humanity is our capacity to differentiate between these, with every moment inviting the choice to be guided by this universal perspective. This is the renaissance, and it is coming. Before releasing the arrow, however, we must remember that we are in uncharted waters, without a map. We are living in possibly the most exciting time ever to be alive and our young people and those entering adulthood will release the shame and fear of the generational trauma that living out of alignment with our true nature has evoked. As both older and younger generations, we are waking up, cleaning up, growing up and showing up. We need to do the Fosbury flop of perspective and go beyond our collective conditioning and the stories we have been told so that we can flourish in a new age when the workplace will be characterized by an individual's capacity to contribute to a united good. Gen Z consumers are already demanding coherence from companies and brands with their purchasing power, and this mentality will express further into the workplace as we start to recognize just how out of kilter our corporate structures have become in the last century.

As the arrow takes flight, let us remember that we are all far greater than we could ever imagine. The invitation here is to become intimate with who you are in relationship to your nature as nature, to the rhythm of the seasons, the moon and the sun and the power of the planets in relationship to yourself. It is okay to set high standards for ourselves, as long as in doing so we are an example of what it means to be fully human, to live in wholeness and coherence and to serve humanity in the humane economy we are creating.

> 'Let your bending in the archer's hand be for gladness: For even as He loves the arrow that flies, so He loves also the bow that is stable.'
>
> Kahlil Gibran[3]

What I now know

Ask yourself: Who am I? and Who does life want me to be?

Do not look for an employer to fulfil your cravings. Do your own 'Work' to better understand who you really are. Not your identity or conditioning and stories you tell yourself for validation, but who you really are at a soul level. Once you know the answer, this frequency when expressed in the world will take form in your life.

Be courageous enough to know, at the deepest part of yourself, what is best for you. Be discerning – always. Don't be fooled by others and don't fool yourself.

The real truth about life during these ambiguous times is that being courageous is not about becoming a Spitfire ace and fighting for your country like my grandfather did. Yes, the same big, open heart is required, but that heart and commitment to service will not be given away to your country in war. It is yours to share with a higher authority for peace and the preservation of humanity and the realization of the interconnection of all things. So, align your creative life force with the higher authority that exists within yourself as together we build the 'house of tomorrow'.

Bring to mind the following ten point plan to become Un:Stuck and to help you navigate difficult moments

1 Know yourself.
2 Listen to your heart and the inner guidance of your true self.
3 Distinguish between your true self and your ego.
4 Your ego is your identity; your awareness is your connection.
5 Be discerning about what you consume with your eyes, ears and senses.
6 Realize you are a frequency interacting with energy.
7 Express your authentic Self, not your conditioned self.
8 Allow your frequency to guide you towards an aligned community.
9 Surrender to life and don't be attached to outcomes.
10 Set an example of coherence rather than tell others what to do.

To quote the seventeenth-century Japanese poet and Zen master Matsuo Bashō:

> Do not seek to follow in the footsteps of the wise; seek what they sought. Seek the meaning behind their footsteps, and not upon the steps themselves. For in seeking the footsteps you shall be glancing only upon the next footprint. And you're sure to stumble upon an unforeseen obstacle. But in seeking the meaning behind their footsteps you're sure to see ahead; comparable to looking up while walking. Thus, allowing you to easily manoeuvre around the hurdles on the path you walk.
>
> ...And if you walk like this long enough, you'll one day, to your surprise, find yourself among the wise.[4]

Om Namo Narayani I bow to this Ultimate Reality.

Key action points for parents and providers of care

First, ask yourself, 'Who am I (really)?' – not 'What have I achieved?' Then, remind your children and those in your care to do the same.

We are living in possibly the most exciting time ever to be alive. Let us be an example of what it means to be fully human, to live in wholeness and to come together, and work together, for a united good.

Remind our younger generation that they are the architects of their own realities, which are unlimited. But only by talking openly, honestly and deeply with them can we help them tune into what the deepest part of them knows.

Let us remind ourselves, and our young people, that we *all* have the neural wiring for awakened awareness, and as years of research are now confirming, having a spiritual core or believing in some form of higher power is the most powerful factor for overcoming the rising waves of despair in our world. In other words, we can live chasing goals and rewards, lost in worries and regrets, or we can focus more on our inner values and awaken to a deeply felt alignment with life.

Always remember that there is a way to do things better – and our role is to help the younger generation find their unique path, so they can live more closely aligned with their hearts, their spiritual essence and nature as nature.

Notes

1. Gibran, Kahlil, *The Prophet*. Knopf, 1923.
2. De Chardin, Pierre Teilhard 'The evolution of chastity', in *Toward the Future*. Harcourt 1936.
3. Gibran, Kahlil, *The Prophet*. Knopf, 1923.
4. Jami, Quoted in Criss, *Killosophy*, CreateSpace Independent Publishing Platform, 2015.

9

Diving deep: my journey to self-discovery and Oceanic Global

Lea d'Auriol

'No Blue, No Green.'

Sylvia Earle

The path of activism is a deeply personal one and in this profoundly moving story, Oceanic Global founder Lea d'Auriol shares her journey through loss, trauma, courage and self-discovery that fueled her work as a young activist. Through her story, she empowers us, young and old alike, to translate our frustrations and despair into clarity for the future and to renew our relationships with ourselves, with Earth, and with life.

We are all sailors navigating our respective lives. The reality is that most of us born today are born into a storm. My life is no exception. It is full of awe and joy, but also of hardship. In balancing this duality, I am learning to surrender and to trust. I have chosen to believe that my life is unfolding exactly as it should and that I have had, and continue to have, hard lessons to learn; that going through pain teaches me more about myself and how best to show up as my whole self for others, for the ocean and for all life on Earth.

My work has taken form through a non-profit called Oceanic Global, which I founded in 2016. Oceanic Global reminds us of humanity's original role in Earth's broader ecosystems and guides us in restoring equilibrium to our blue planet. Our core focus areas are designed to deepen humanity's connection to the ocean as the lifeblood of the Earth, to provide tangible solutions for resilience and to create blueprints for coexisting in harmony with our natural world.

The organization is both a manifestation of the lessons I have learned from life's ebbs and flows and a compass that always points me back towards my purpose, most especially when rougher waters arise. By sharing my story of how Oceanic Global came to be, I hope it will help others who may be struggling to navigate their own journey, while also inspiring those exploring their own activism to show up as their true selves and help contribute to life in ways that feel most meaningful to them.

My story

So let me start at the beginning – with my self-identity. I have always viewed myself as a child of the world, in that for a very long time, I struggled with feeling that there was no place in particular where I truly belonged. I was born and grew up in Hong Kong, China, and was raised in a bilingual household. My father is a Frenchman from Paris and my mother was English. Her family was of fourth generation born in India, a country which I had never been. To be honest, the first time I felt a keen sense of 'belonging' was in my mid-twenties. After founding Oceanic Global, I had the strong and incredibly grounding realization that, regardless of geographical lines and other societal structures, I was fundamentally a part of nature, and as an inhabitant of the Earth, I, like all human, was as welcome in the world as any other being.

From then on, whenever I felt limited because of my lack of roots in one specific land, I remembered my, and humanity's, innate connection to water. Covering over 70 per cent of the planet and constituting more than 95 per cent of the biosphere, the ocean not only connects all continents, but also connects us with one another. After all, close to 60 per cent of our bodies are made up of the same water that makes up most of the world.

Understanding this interconnectedness with water and the inter-connectedness of humans to water has strengthened my sense of belonging within the web of life. After all, the definition of 'oceanic' is of, living in or produced by the ocean – and I believe that humanity is oceanic and it is an identity that we all share.

Just as discovering this sense of commonality helped me navigate feelings of not belonging to one country or culture, it also gifted me the ability to build bridges between worlds. Whether it is working on the ground with local communities and knowledge holders, engaging in creative design, participating in the business world or being involved in institutional settings, I have found my unique way of building bridges and bringing people together. This perspective is reflected in the core of our work at Oceanic Global, where we prioritize a multi-disciplinary approach, acting as a bridge and providing local solutions and resources in the 55 countries we operate in, as well as through our work with the United Nations hosting World Oceans Day since 2019.

Growing up in Hong Kong also helped cultivate my love of nature, while also drawing attention to the inherent dangers of modern societies. Hong Kong is one of the planet's most vibrant and cosmopolitan cities and is filled with myriad paradoxes. Yet, in a city that is powered by development, the population suffers from high levels of air pollution, as well as dangerous levels of ocean pollution that would sometimes render certain beaches inaccessible. Nevertheless, Hong Kong remains a magical and unique place, not just a city but a region made up of over 2,000 islands, which once comprised more than 50 per cent natural park protected lands – spaces where my love of and connection with nature and water were born and nurtured.

My childhood weekends were spent at sea – sailing, swimming and exploring the vast coastlines with my cousins and siblings. Together we would dream in nature, acting out endless stories around mermaid rocks. The ocean was and still is my happy place. It is the place I go to play, to recharge and to feel inspired by life. I am so fortunate to have enjoyed this extraordinary childhood, filled with the freedom to explore and to be constantly inspired by the world around me. My love for the outdoors and dreaming provided an escape from school, where I struggled with dyslexia at a time when most schools did not provide the tools for children to learn differently. While at the time that struggle felt like a disadvantage, it was also instrumental in teaching me to find my own way and to build resilience, and it gave me the confidence to speak my own voice.

Before I was ten years old, I experienced how delicate our human interactions with nature are and how we were negatively impacting some of Earth's most pristine ecosystems: in the same Hong Kong waters I swam in we discovered there were pink dolphins that were at risk of extinction. This extreme of loving the ocean and all its beauty while also realizing that as humans we were fast destroying these fragile and fundamental ecosystems marked me greatly.

In contrast to Hong Kong's abundance of nature is the grim socio-economic inequality evident throughout South-East Asia. My mother worked tirelessly to help mitigate this, spending her time helping in elderly homes in Hong Kong to campaigning for children and burn victims in Nepal. From a young age, my siblings and I volunteered once a week for the Child Welfare Scheme, a charity doing amazing work in Nepal, and I knew that being involved in non-profits would undoubtedly become a key part of my future. I was dedicated, even then, to doing what I felt was needed to make the world a better and more just place.

My mother was an artist at heart and a very spiritual and open role model. My father was a businessman. He was reliable, strong, compassionate and always wanted us to be independent. Together, they instilled in us three children the need to learn and to contribute to society in our own unique ways. This meant doing summer internships from the age of 14. Regardless of what it was, we needed to experience life. Like many, I felt the pressure of being asked by adults what I was going to do when I 'grew up' and the frustration of having no clear idea at the time. I was 25 years old when Oceanic Global was created, and it was then that I realized my true purpose in life and how to best show up for it. I share this as I now know that it doesn't actually matter what we do; we just need to start by saying yes to opportunities that can lead us to experience life in ways we would otherwise struggle to comprehend.

When I was 14, my younger brother, Teo, who was just 12, drowned in a swimming pool in Bali. His death flipped my world upside down. I became very angry towards the world and its injustice, contemplating death, life and so much more. Living in Asia and being exposed to Eastern philosophies from a young age, I was fortunate to have grown up with a strong spiritual connection, so I began searching for meaning in life as it was the only way I could continue to live. A year after Teo's passing, I returned to the place in Bali where he had died to intern as an assistant midwife so I could witness the beginning of life in an area where my brother's life had ended so young. This contrast helped me better understand the delicate balance between life and death. When Teo passed, I chose to live for him and my family. I became a survivor, viewing life as something to overcome rather than truly processing my trauma and living life for the experience and joy of it. This survivor archetype remained with me for over half of my life and it's one that I am still processing today. Among the markings of Teo's passing, I also found the courage and resilience to carry on in the realization that time was short and life was precious, all of which reinforced in me this deep sense of the myriad responsibilities that each of us has in how we choose to show up for ourselves, for one another and for the world at large.

Ten years after Teo died, my mother, Sandra, passed away suddenly in 2014. I was in my early twenties and had just moved to New York for my first full-time job. Yet again, my life flipped, but this time it was different.

I moved home to Hong Kong for three months to help my dad and younger sister, Pia. My mum was many things, among them a jewellery designer. She was greatly loved by so many, and in her honour I organized a sale of her last pieces of jewellery and photographs, so that those who loved her could feel connected to her. All proceeds were donated to various charities, one of which focused on ocean pollution. This was my first deep dive into the inner workings of the non-profit sector, and I quickly learned how they were positioned, where the money was going and how people could get more involved.

I often recall a conversation I had with my mum, three years prior to her passing, when she started working in ocean conservation. I asked her why she chose activism for the ocean when all her work to date had been focused on helping people. She shared with me that the ocean is the foundation of all life on Earth and that to truly help others, we need to take care of nature, as we rely on nature and our oceans to survive. She spoke about how much easier it was to simply hold a photo of a child in front of someone and ask for financial support, but so much harder to do this for the ocean – as so many people did not feel that same connection or understand the pivotal role the ocean plays in sustaining life and regulating climate. She said we needed to speak for those who have forgotten how to listen to the ocean. This conversation, combined with my deep love for the ocean, planted a seed that, unknown to me at that time, would soon germinate.

I contemplated going into the non-profit space then but decided to first pursue a career in a more traditional setting. Moving back to New York I started working with a small events and PR firm. I loved the high-paced life – working long hours with lots of responsibility in my young hands. I learned by doing, and those years gave me an unforgettable foundation and ardent work ethic. Throwing myself into my work and the new friendships left little time for grieving – it was just too painful. However, in contrast to this fast-paced, exciting lifestyle was the reality that event production is one of the most wasteful industries and I soon realized that my work was actually contributing to material waste and fast consumerism.

After an intense almost two years, I went to Ibiza in Spain where I had spent many happy summers with my mother's parents. Ibiza always felt like home, and I arrived this time needing the nourishment and support of the ocean more than ever before.

Sitting on a beach reading an article highlighting how we were just ten years away from our human impact having irreversible damage on the ocean, I remember feeling a profound ache in my heart. I loved the ocean. It was my happy place and in that moment I realized I couldn't lose that too. My grief for the ocean was tied to my grief for my mother and my brother, Teo. I knew that I could not lose anything else I loved as I just didn't know if I could survive.

Oceanic Global came to me in that moment, and while we all have many great ideas, the difference was this was the one that I chose to act on. It felt and still feels like the most important thing to me. Having grown up seeing first-hand how destructive our human impact on the ocean and the environment really is, I could not understand why people were not doing more to change these destructive ways, especially those of my own generation, the Millennials and youth. That night, I dreamed up our first event for for Oceanic Global. I didn't realize then that I was using the skills I learned after my mother died to create a non-profit – all I did know was that I needed to create an event supporting ocean conservation that would bring people together and inspire them to act on behalf of the ocean.

One week later, back in New York, I shared my idea with my two best friends, both of whom I worked with. 'Yes, we're in' was their immediate response. We often joke about it now as none of us really knew what 'being in' would really mean! Natasha joked that she would do the PR for free, helping me create my first deck and putting our inaugural mission statement into words. Seven years on, she is a board member and an instrumental part of Oceanic Global. While I was petrified knowing that this was a bold concept, what we lacked in resources and experience we made up for with passion, heart and drive – that combined culminated in the Oceanic x Ibiza event in July 2017.

Oceanic Global officially became a non-profit in 2016 but it wasn't until 2020 that the charity became my full-time work. I share this simply because I don't believe there is any one way to start something. It's simply about starting, failing and restarting – which is the norm for many in this sector. There are many ways to create something.

The reality is we moved so quickly and were constantly in flow that we never stopped to fully comprehend what we were building. I say 'we' as Oceanic Global is much more than me: it comprises many passionate people (including volunteers) who share a love for the ocean and the planet, and who have come together at different phases and given it the love, energy and commitment that have made it what it is today. Those people I work with and continue to build with are what keep me going. Their passion and willingness to contribute is where I find my hope in humanity, and I am lucky enough to have experienced this in the hundreds, if not thousands, of people who have contributed to Oceanic Global in their own way. This has taught me so much, but most of all I have learned that when you ignite a passion within yourself, it lights a path for others – and in following those paths, we are never alone.

Soon after having the idea of Oceanic x Ibiza I was introduced to Karin Isken, who had been working in the cosmetic and textile space for over 30 years. Touched by a desire to mobilize ocean action in Ibiza, she wanted to help us bring this first-of-a-kind event to life. Not only was she an instrumental part of the team, but she also fulfilled her own passion for empowering sustainable change and providing environmental business solutions. After Oceanic x Ibiza, she created a sustainable product and consulting company, helping transition businesses across Europe away from single-use plastics and becoming an Oceanic Global Blue Standard consultant. Karin is one of the many individuals who found their path after realizing the importance of taking environmental action. She continues to impact me greatly and is a constant reminder of how being true to yourself can help awaken the truth in others around you.

My journey with Oceanic Global has been an exploration of life and nature, as well as a road to healing. Driven by my passion and dedication, it has filled my life with an abundance of growth by stimulating my creativity and intellectuality, while also providing deeper meaning to the world and pushing me out of my comfort zone on a daily basis. Most of all it has given me a deep sense of purpose and has forced me to embrace change (something I was always fearful of).

The journey has not been easy as we have faced many hurdles along the way. I still have days where the problems we are working to resolve feel completely overwhelming, but the difference now is that I honour those days and moments as parts of the cycles of life. I have learned to allow myself the time to recuperate, and the space and acknowledgement to feel into my anxieties before they become overbearing. Finding that balance, especially within the space of environmental action, is so important.

As so much of how I show up in life is poured into Oceanic Global, the lessons I have learned personally merge with it too. My deeply rooted survivor mode gave me the strength to create the non-profit in the first place and to push through the many challenges I faced. That said, in recent years I have spent time in deeply personal work that has helped deter me from operating from the survivor mindset that became very much a part of me some years earlier, and as I continue to integrate more of my learnings, I now know that there is more strength in living with flexibility and flow, in embracing change, and in choosing to create from a place of hope and love rather than one of fear. I do not say this lightly as the environmental and climate narrative is heavy and continues to dishearten me as I witness how the majority of people continue to act in the face of current environmental issues. It takes great discipline and courage to feel this but not get completely swept up in the fear narrative, instead acting and creating from a place of love.

Internal healing and planetary healing are inherently connected. My belief is that, as we reconnect with nature, we allow the space for deep healing and the opportunity to feel nourished so we can continue to act on behalf of all life. We are living in a time where we need to build bridges that unite our differences so that together we can reimagine how we should contribute to society and to life. Now is the time for meaningful action.

At Oceanic Global, we work to touch hearts through mediums like art, wellness, innovation and science, while also empowering action through programmes such as our educational campaigns, cross-industry Blue Standard, community grants, regional hubs and global initiatives like United Nations World Oceans Day – all designed to create solutions that can be applied and scaled across all sectors of society in all corners of the world.

I am still young (33), and I know my path as an activist will continue to evolve, as it should – as does everything. I typically don't like labels as I feel we often tend to project our own lived experiences onto them, often to the exclusion of others, but I am proud to call myself an activist. I am deeply honoured to be working with nature, water and the ocean, and I believe we have a collective responsibility and need to come back into balance with them.

What continues to give me hope is knowing that each of us has gifts and perspectives that are entirely unique and that every person on Earth has the potential to create change in their own way. There is so much collective untapped potential that when activated and guided towards a purpose has the power to compound and build a better world.

I encourage everyone reading *Un:Stuck*, regardless of your age and circumstance, to ask yourselves the following:

- How am I showing up in the world and what do I want to represent?
- How can I show up as my true self and stand in my power?
- What are my needs?
- What brings me joy and meaning?
- What is my relationship with nature and the ocean?
- What are the three things I can do now to make the world a more harmonious place?

I believe in humanity and our capacity to evolve. In asking ourselves these questions, we can begin to remember and relearn our role as custodians of this blue planet we all call Earth.

10

Courage: letters to humanity by father and daughter holders of contemporary wisdom, Mindahi and Xiye Bastida

Mindahi Bastida

'Mother Earth is speaking. Mother Earth is crying, but she still has lots of love towards us. We've got to listen. It's not just about willingness, not anymore. It's about responsibility.'

Mindahi Bastida

A letter to my daughter

Dear Xiye,

We are living in prophetic times. We know it is not easy; it is not comfortable, but it's a great opportunity.

It is a great opportunity because once we acknowledge that these times were foreseen by our ancestors, we can make time to pause and connect with them. Without letting judgement get in the way, we can begin to see and feel our ancestors closer rather than as distant family, who thought a lot about the future and that of their future children. With love and intention, we can open our hearts to what they wish to pass on. At this point they may grant words of wisdom and advice, and most importantly they may bring memories of original landscapes and of the art of working with the natural world of the seen and the unseen. These memories will bring clarity and guidance as to what we have come to be and what we are here to do.

Furthermore, this reconnection with our ancestors and their worldview induces a reconnection with the cosmos and Mother Earth, integrating the spiritual and material worlds within us and dissipating the fear and anxiety that surround the purpose of our lives.

During these times of increasing aggression and dysfunctional relationships at home, in school, in community centres, in workspaces and natural spaces, and at this critical moment in history when the world population has been forced into isolation, we have been shown three fields within which we can experience a sense of empowerment and freedom, and the opportunity to test our collective free determination to become true humans.

The first field is that of digitally and chemically induced reality, where avatars of ourselves become heroes and villains in the virtual reality of screens or inside our minds. This is where the vast majority of our youth are playing, and it reinforces the sense of separation to the point where they are rejecting the tangible world and suppressing any longing for connectedness and any form of expression of emotion.

The second is the field of the tangible natural world, where many forms of life continue to be sustained in urban parks, open nature, care-giving communities (like health centres) or nurture-giving systems (like farms and community gardens). Here, many of our youth have found their place as earthlings within the web of life and have become outspoken and proactive stewards of nature in some kind or form. They work with like-minded people to collectively concentrate their efforts on healing and restoring, while striving to enforce new agreements and rules to ensure long-term socio-ecological balance.

Many who are living in this second field are also cultivating the third field – the space of the loving mind and heart. This sacred space within requires permanent spiritual nurturing through prayers that connect the heart of Father Sky with the heart of Mother Earth.

In Original Peoples' territories where pollution and devastation prevail due to evident acts of ethnocide and ecocide, the great resistance and resiliency of our relatives can only be attributed to a strong spiritual practice. Always remember that this community of relatives includes birds, fish and all creatures that live in prayer, because they repeat beautiful thoughts, acts and practices over and over, while working responsibly towards the care of life in her multiple expressions.

We now have an immense opportunity to recover, restore and co-create communities where there is enduring sustenance of biocultural systems based on the pillars of natural relationships.

For those you meet who might not know where to begin their journey to becoming true humans, people with resilient and courageous hearts and minds, please have them recite these simple words:

'I am not I, I am we.'

As soon as each of us acknowledges that we are a collective, that our minds and hearts connect to all that irradiates beauty and love, we can begin to grow a community of co-creation, restoration and protection for enduring harmony.

This unfolding of the collective self reminds us that there is nothing more corrosive for the soul than to be related to sterile seeds, barren soils, polluted waters, destructive hurricanes and orphaned families, be they eagles, trees, elephants, whales or humans.

Everyone has talents, but these are not gifts, they are responsibilities, and it is time for you, Xiye, to meet your responsibilities, now.

Disconnection from the natural world and disconnection from family and community are the greatest challenges faced by humanity. We must always remember that we are not alone. Our ancestors are the roots – they are guiding us – they are the rivers and seas. They are the mountains, the stars and all that exists in the natural world. We must remember that we are all together – we have to reconnect and remember who we are.

We must take care of our bodies because our body is our sacred vase. If we really take care of our thoughts and think beautifully, this energy gives us enough strength for our spirit to revitalize our body. This spirit is not ours – it is the universe. We are connected. We are never alone. We are survivors of colonization and the modern way of living and yet, we are here.

What is happening to us? Have we forgotten that we are just humans? We are not the peak of creation. We are just another species. We must behave in such a way and we must observe the laws of nature and the universe. And remember the original instructions for the care of life.

We are living through very critical times. If we want to really respect life, we have to acknowledge the spirit of other beings, the spirit of the mountain, the spirit of the river, the spirit of the sea, the spirit of Father Sky and the spirit of the world, Mother Earth.

> We have to go from the I to the We.
>
> From the Me to the We.
>
> It is the time. And that is the reason we are here.

We are not just praying for and caring for the 80 per cent of the world's biodiversity that has been acknowledged recently by international organizations and governments. We are caring for Mother Earth and Father Sky. It's not just biodiversity. It's biocultural heritage and biocultural diversity as we don't distinguish between nature and culture. Biocultural heritage is the significance that a culture gives to nature, while also reminding us of the interweaving of nature and culture.

It is our belief that water is not a resource; it is a sacred element. The air is a sacred element, the earth too, and the wind and the fire. They need to exist for life to flourish. If we must intervene in natural processes, let us do so with respect and utmost consideration for Mother Earth and restrain ourselves from taking more than we need or with disproportionate harm.

As humans we need clean energies, but remember that the most abundant and efficient energy source is solar, which becomes transformed into the natural organisms that exist and abound. There is plenty of space for everyone. We are just another species – we are the syntheses of all that exists – and we need to remember that we are one in diversity.

We must also remember that our ancestors conceived time as cyclical according to the laws of nature and we must follow Nature's way. This is important because we must apply and can teach others to apply the following principles in all of our lives:

- **Slow down:** when we follow the pace of the natural cycles, we are given the opportunity to slow down and to take only as much as can naturally be replenished. This leads us to plan with responsibility and care. For instance, we observe what food systems can provide without excessive input of water, energy and infrastructure, and to exchange products within local and regional scales only.
- **Scale down:** living in accordance with the natural cycles leads us to value each thing that we have, that we eat and that we need. But it also helps us to realize that when we don't have immediate access to things, we can better understand how much we rely on ready availability and so many other things that are not necessary. Many of us, city people in particular, have been led to believe that life is about acquiring as much 'stuff' as possible. But we, as consumers,

must understand the repercussions of our choices and be more educated about where things are sourced from, what geography and season they come from, and how we can reduce the volume of 'stuff' we acquire. All of this will naturally reduce the pressure on ecosystems and local communities.

- **Wind down**: people, companies, investors and communities need to see themselves moving forward in creative, cyclical ways, not in straight lines. Linear timelines lead people to see their life as one of either success or failure, most especially when success is defined by the accumulation of wealth and the making of profit. When forced by nature to slow down and scale down, we are being given a chance to live more simple lives and to be happy with less. Those companies that keep thinking of profit as the most relevant aspect of economic models will probably not respond fast enough to the new value systems of consumers – a system where rivers have rights and the Earth has rights – to their own demise.

When conceiving projects in a circular and spiral manner, outcomes occur in stages. For us, as Original Peoples, life happens within cycles of expanded regeneration, where there is sprouting, learning, maturing, reproducing and also giving away, to avoid accumulation and to enable new sprouting.

We also have the opportunity to adjust our pace to the rhythms of nature's cycles, drafting new life plans that are designed not as a function of exponential accumulation of capital for personal satisfaction but rather as a function of regenerative and resilient complex living systems. This adjustment in the pace and speed at which we participate in taking, processing, distributing, exchanging, disposing, and recirculating energy and materials, both as consumers and providers, requires some introspection regarding the mindset that has driven Western societies to get up every morning. For too long it has been the competitive 'survival of the fittest' and the selfish, greedy, mistrusting, linear thinking, enslaving and patriarchal mindset. Avoid these patterns of behaviour and learn to differentiate between those initiatives that are deeply transformational and others that are replicating old models in sophisticated disguise.

This is my prayer to you, Xiye, and to all of humanity:

We give great thanks to the Great Spirit for allowing us to remember the original instructions to be in this world. We give great thanks to the four sacred elements of life. We give great thanks to our ancestors and the seeds for the flourishing of life. We give great thanks for having this experience, time and space and to remember that we are one in diversity. We call for the raise of consciousness in the care of life and the transcendence of it.

Kjamadi, may love be among us.

Your loving father,
Mindahi

Xiye Bastida

'The youth run the fastest, but the elders know the path.'

African proverb

When I was around four years old I would ask my dad why the world was unjust. I would ask why our air was contaminated. I would ask him to explain why it hurt my lungs when I took a deep breath by our river and why the apples of Grandma's apple tree wouldn't produce seeds. He said that things were out of balance and that it was our purpose on this Earth to bring balance back. It was our task to give back to Mother Earth. It was our duty to fight, so that all fights could end. It took me a long time to understand this, and I still forget sometimes.

I feel the pain of the Earth when I see a tree trapped between two highways. I feel the pain of the Earth when I see miles and miles of cities covering once thriving land. But I also feel the resilience of Mother Earth. I see the flowers and the grass growing in between pavement cracks and I hear birds singing in the heart of the biggest cities in the world. What my dad told me unleashed my imagination: *we are here to bring balance back.* So I imagined justice, I imagined beauty, I imagined harmony and I imagined fulfilling the dreams of my ancestors.

If it was up to me, the world would have changed in an instant. If it was up to me, all trees would be allowed to grow and all rivers would be allowed to flow and change. If it was up to me, all humans would know what it feels like to put our face on the damp earth or the damp sand. But to my surprise, my imagined world was called naive. And I said to myself, 'Don't they see the rivers losing their roots? Don't they see the clouds losing their way? Don't they see the Sun, bright red, begging us to wake up?'

The modern world almost changed me. I almost believed I had to accept 'the real world'. But then I thought, everything that we see was thought of and built by someone. Our thoughts weren't beautiful and our spirit wasn't pure when we invented mines and oil flaring, or mass consumption, or extreme waste. I realized that the world I imagined was possible because I was going to bring it into existence.

With my new-found clarity, I was ready to change the world, so I embarked on the journey of talking to people who supposedly knew 'how the world worked' about how in fact it didn't work! But they would ask me questions I didn't understand, not because I couldn't conceptualize them but because they were out of sync with a world of thriving life.

Every time I was confused about the world – about someone's outlook or about someone's actions – I would ask my dad, 'Why?' And somehow, he always had the right answer. That's when I understood that, even though I have all the energy and inclination to change the world, I cannot do it without his wisdom. I cannot do it without the willing hearts and willing hands of those who run global institutions and define what the world is today. Only then can we work together on and conceptualize of the world of tomorrow.

For the past six years I have been giving all my time, energy and love to the climate justice movement – it is something that is born so deep within me that I can't help it. It gives me joy and purpose. But in the midst of the fast-paced lifestyle I had been living, I had forgotten to breathe deeply more often. I forgot that what the world needs is for us to slow down. And before you can ask that of someone else, you must first practise it yourself.

Clarity only comes with reflection, and reflection can only happen when you give yourself time to really connect with Mother Earth. For this connection to happen, we must give back – a prayer – a craft – a ceremony. All of us need to start giving back to Mother Earth so she can then speak to us and through us. Then we will move forward with strength.

A letter to my father

Dear Dad,

In recent days I've remembered when I was little. I write these lines to you with great feeling and gratitude. Together with Mom, you have taught me to love life since before I was born. You raised me in a world of songs, games, books, talks and walks. All of this made my imagination travel far and wide. When I was a child I liked to lie on your chest, as listening to your heartbeat connected me with the harmony of the universe.

I barely knew how to say many words when you were already taking me by the hand through the fields and forests. There you taught me to see the colours of butterflies and to touch the different textures of stones and leaves. The trees seemed huge to me, but when I said I wanted to climb them and reach high up, you lifted me onto firm branches, helping me remain steady. As I grew older, that self-confidence allowed me to ride a horse, ride a bicycle, balance myself on the gymnastics bar and stand on a stage with a microphone for the first time, without hesitation. You and Mom have given me the confidence and trust, and you continue to remind me to remember to always be in connection and gratitude with Makihmu, the Great Spirit.

On walks in the mountains as a girl with my little brother, the birds and their songs, the winds among the leaves, and the guardians of the forest and caves... everything was an awakening of my senses and imagination. Thank you for that deep connection with the mysterious. In the little green house, where we prepared the biointensive beds, it was wonderful to work with the soil and feel that it was alive thanks to so many worms, and it was great to see that all the plants were happy with the compost-rich soil.

Since I can remember, I always saw you and Mom with books on the table, studying and talking about the wetland, the Laguna Chimaliapan. Later I learned that, since the year I was born (2002), the Lerma Wetlands Flora and Fauna Protection Area has existed, thanks to you. Through this you taught me that when you persist, when you put in all your might, you can achieve big dreams.

I also remember when you attended community assemblies to share your vision of revitalizing the Lerma Wetlands. You and my grandfather have a special love for the Laguna Chimaliapan. My grandfather always gave his life to defend it alongside other locals, as it is a communal territory. Whether the duties of guarding the land are scheduled for the day or the night, my grandfather has always been there, while he had the physical strength. I see in my grandfather this perseverance and courage to defend the land, and I admire him because, despite his age, he has put his whole heart into leaving the legacy of the wetland to his children.

You tell me about the mermaid as the mother of the waters and you also tell me about when my grandfather went out at three in the morning to cut the tule to make the mats and other crafts. These are pieces that sustain the identity of the family, the community and the territory. The defence of the wetland and the land guarantees the perpetuity of life, and it is how we can ensure that our cultural roots grow deeper, that stems and fruits emerge and that seeds can give again.

You have also taught me that we are here in this world to take care of life. It is so beautiful to remember the first time we went to the wetland, where I saw the bulrush, the herons, the ducks and many aquatic plants. Ensuring the survival of the *ciénegas* (wetland systems) shows the love you have for the culture of our ancestors and for the children who will come in the future. Together we observed how the wetland has defended itself from desiccation works; it has been resilient, remaining over time despite the excessive extraction of water from the aquifer and the serious contamination to which it has been subjected for more than four decades. This not only tells us that resilience is a human quality but also that ecosystems in their entirety can experience it.

Among other things, you have also taught me that we must build alliances with those who share the same aspirations and principles, which are to take care of life, and that together we are stronger and can achieve things more effectively. And that, during these times, we have to be responsible and help in the regeneration of life through a reconnection with nature that will enrich our biocultural heritage.

Dad, I am also very grateful that you have taught me to respect Elders and to see with love everything that surrounds us. This love cultivates in people a collective personality, which means that one starts to think of oneself as 'We' and not anymore as 'I'.

It is necessary to create circles of dialogue between Elders and young people so together we can strengthen and maintain thought and action in the defence and care of life. I am still young and I am constantly learning, and I know that your ancestral wisdom sustains me and sustains us all in this world because that wisdom respects the laws of origin, the laws of nature and the laws of the universe. And most importantly, it is what will persist over time, even if modern life denies us the benefits of being wise in this world.

Finally, I want to thank you for this important message that has expanded with your teachings: that we should take only what is necessary and that we should live 'with' life: with Earth and not 'off' the Earth, and that like a mother, this Earth loves us, but that we must return that love through our actions, in reciprocity.

You have wisely said that Earth can live without us, but we cannot live without her. We are in this world to serve, but it is not about serving from the human to the human. We must not serve by thinking 'what world we are leaving for those who come next' but rather what humans we are leaving for Mother Earth. That is the sacred co-responsibility that you have taught me: it is about maintaining, respecting, guarding and observing the actions of caring in the collective state of being with beautiful Mother Earth and Father Sky.

Thank you, Dad, for passing on to me the legacy and wisdom of our Otomi-Toltec lineage.

Kjamadi – may love be among us.
Xiye

11

Finding myself: one breath at a time

Ryan Dusick

'Sit there, stop, be yourself first, and begin from there.'

Thich Nhat Hanh[1]

I used to think pop stars who cancelled tours due to 'exhaustion' were simply being divas or were downplaying a major drug or alcohol problem... until it happened to me.

As a young man following my dreams of becoming a rock star, I was possessed by a passionate commitment to my love of music, my deep connection with my bandmates and my fervent pursuit of a career at the highest levels of music performance. These sources of meaning and purpose propelled me and my group forward for a decade, until we finally achieved our dreams of global stardom as Maroon 5. This drive for success ultimately consumed me; the lifestyle of a touring musician became detrimental to my physical and mental health.

The relentless touring in support of our breakthrough album, *Songs about Jane*, eventually caught up with me. We were in the middle of a four-year, worldwide promotional campaign, during which we were instructed to 'say yes to everything', and any breaks in our schedule quickly evaporated as our album climbed the pop charts. And just when it was time to enjoy the rewards of our success, my body and mind gave out. The breakdown that ensued proved devastating, not only to my career but to the very fabric of my being, as I fell into a tailspin of depression, anxiety and alcoholism that lasted a decade.

After quitting drinking in 2016, I finally found new connection and purpose, turning what had been a personal tragedy into triumph and redemption. During this time I discovered passions for service and mental health, which inspired me to pursue a whole new life and career as a psychotherapist, advocate and author of *Harder to Breathe: A memoir of making Maroon 5, losing it all, and finding recovery*.

The greatest remedy for my loss of identity was to create new meaning and fulfilment in my life – a journey that brought deeper contentment than I ever could have thought possible. And the work I do now has been equally, if not even more, fulfilling than creating music and performing. That said, I will never know what could have been because the pressures of performing wore me down to such an extent that continuing was no longer an option.

When I look back on that younger version of myself, touring endlessly in support of our multi-platinum, breakthrough album, I see a precocious young man with a lot of great things going for him, but lacking the tools to cope with his deeply ingrained insecurities and anxieties. At the time, my greatest challenges came in the form of perfectionism, obsessive-compulsiveness, self-doubt and imposter syndrome as I worked through an unrelenting schedule of travel and performance for almost four years straight. It wasn't until after the breakdown that I started to understand the real depths of my anxiety.

I wish I had known back then that I wasn't alone, that we all have insecurities and vulnerabilities, and the first step in overcoming them is acknowledging and expressing them. Even super-confident people have some level of self-doubt or self-criticism inside of them. Often these people hold the deepest insecurities. It's basic psychology – a defence mechanism. If you had known me as a young man, you never would have guessed that I struggled so much with anxiety and self-doubt. On the outside I appeared to have it all together, but inside I was constantly burying vulnerable feelings, never allowing myself to express the negative thoughts or ask anyone for help. And naturally, this plan of defence just made matters worse. Perhaps if I had given myself an outlet for my emotions, I could have gained the much-needed support and guidance to bring relief from the intense pressures.

I learned the hard way that ignoring a problem, or just pushing it further down, doesn't make it go away. The avoided issue comes back, stronger every time. But as a successful young man, I didn't want to hear that. I wanted to believe that I could just push it out of my mind and try ever harder to control the things that were slipping from my grasp. It was only years later, when I finally began to sit with and work through the discomfort, that I finally started to overcome these anxieties. Yes, this process was scary at first, but it became less so once I began to face my insecurities head on. For me and many others like me, the only way through the anxiety... is through it!

I also wish I had known back then that self-care is the most important and *most productive* element of any lifestyle, regardless of how busy, stressed or in demand you believe yourself to be. In fact, it becomes even more important when you're living under increasing pressure. That's when those life-saving tools help you remain centred, balanced and, most importantly, healthy. Self-care isn't complex; it's exactly as it sounds: taking good care of yourself by nourishing your body, prioritizing rest and sleep, getting good exercise, and feeding your mind and spirit with healthy connections and quality relationships. When all of these parts are in alignment, daily challenges become much easier to navigate and coping with anxiety and stress becomes less overwhelming.

Living a healthy lifestyle is a constant for me now: I eat well, exercise daily, prioritize connection and purpose, and I play softball every Sunday morning, mostly because it reminds me of what it feels like to do something purely for the joy of it (while also embracing and nourishing my inner child!). And although it's not onstage in front of thousands of people anymore, I play music for fun, simply because it feels good to sing and move to a groove. I also take time to sit in the present moment, without dwelling too heavily on disappointments from the past or fixating too intensely on things that might cause me discomfort in the future. And I invest myself in challenges that offer me fulfilment – so much so that I find myself walking towards the things that make me uncomfortable, knowing that the opportunity for growth lies in those things that challenge me most.

My daily practice of mindfulness continues to keep me grounded. To this end, Jon Kabat-Zinn's *Full Catastrophe Living* has been a great support as it offers a comprehensive description of the mindset, attitudes and practice of mindful living.[2] Every morning I foster a relationship with the present moment through mindful stretching, mindful breathing and radical acceptance of what *is*. I have found this practice pulls me out of past regrets and alleviates my tendency to ruminate on 'what-ifs' about the future.

When confronted with moments of anxiety, I attempt to tune into the reality of the situation. I now know that what is happening during these moments is often far less concerning than what I tend to project onto them. If I just take a few minutes to realign my perception with what is actually occurring, I can clear away and reframe any negative judgements I may have superimposed. By practising radical acceptance of what *is* rather than attempting to control or change things, I free myself from the frustrations and reactivity that arise from overthinking.

I am truly blessed to have found a second act in my life, but many others have not been so fortunate. Anxiety, depression, substance abuse and other mental health challenges have led to outcomes far worse than the loss of a performing career. So, I would much rather see a talented young artist take time out to find balance and wellness in a long and thriving career than see them shine brightly for a short time before burning out completely.

The best advice I can give to young people is to stay open to change. As scary as it may seem, change is what allows us to grow and improve. Sometimes things get worse before they get better, but if we keep walking in the direction of progress and growth, eventually we notice that life becomes a little easier and brighter. It's also very important to take a few moments to acknowledge progress. Perfection is an illusion, but progress is slow and steady. By staying open and teachable, we allow the possibilities to unfold in time. We notice and embrace the opportunities as they arise rather than dismissing them as threats to be avoided. By adopting this mindset of growth, we begin to see every challenge as an opportunity to learn and improve.

The best advice I can give to parents, teachers and caregivers of young people is to take the time to really *listen* – rather than immediately jumping to advice or 'fixing'. What these young people want and need above all else is to feel seen, heard and understood. Often the greatest gift we can give is to show them that we are truly listening, that we hear what they are saying and that we empathize with their feelings. Don't be afraid to ask questions and then reflect back what you have heard them say about their inner experience. By allowing them to express themselves, you are offering them the opportunity to discover their own pathways towards growth and change.

When we feel listened to, when we know that our feelings matter, and when we say aloud those things we have bottled up inside, the healing process begins.

Notes

1. Hanh, Thich Nhat, *Peace is Every Step: The path of mindfulness in everyday life*. Rider, 1991.
2. Kabat-Zinn, Jon, *Full Catastrophe Living: How to cope with stress, pain and illness using mindfulness meditation*. Pitakus, 2013.

12

Finding flow

Dr Easkey Britton

'Even in the vast and mysterious reaches of the sea we are brought back to the fundamental truth that nothing lives to itself.'

Rachel Carson, *Silent Spring*[1]

Those who immerse themselves in cold water know of its extraordinary ability to connect us more closely with our bodies and our sense of self. My life is lived by the tides and the cycle of the Moon. From my home in Donegal on Ireland's wild Atlantic north-west coastline, I can hear the storms arriving from the Atlantic during the night. I plan my day around tide charts and predicted swell heights so that I can always make myself available to the ocean. It means my schedule often doesn't comply with linear time, which can sometimes cause problems in a society hooked on hyper-productivity, but my ocean connection gives me balance and keeps me grounded.

During these times of such wild uncertainty, the ocean, with the ebb and flow of its tides, is a place of constancy for me. The ocean teaches me to be fully present with what is, and what pulls me most, I guess, is the clarity – trusting the process – which for me is less about trying to change things and more about how we choose to be with the way things are. This has come from years of the salt water leaving its residue on my skin until I feel I too am part water.

As a surfer and marine social scientist, I'm enthralled by waves. Waves are shaped by the wind, a beautiful reminder of the complex beauty of how the unseen forces of nature work; the energetic friction between storm-driven winds and the surface of the open ocean, causing a build-up of energy that begins to ripple outwards and deepen into ocean swells marching across the sea until meeting a continental shelf and shallow coastal waters – the bathymetry shaping these swells into waves causing them to rise, steepen, curl, peel and crash onto the shore.

For many, the sea remains an expanse of 'blue space'. What lies below the surface most humans may never see or experience first-hand.

I had the good fortune of a childhood spent in close proximity to the coast, full of the wonder of tidal movements, the power of the sea and fast-moving weather fronts. At a very early age I learned about the life of intertidal zones from time spent in rock pools, before following my mother and father into the surf. I learned through surfing the importance of paying attention to natural processes, flows and rhythms, all well beyond human control.

The sea is the great mother, supporting all life on Earth. Most of the water in the ocean today was formed 4 billion years ago. This ancient sea is also where the first life on Earth began. Our bodies are up to 60 per cent salt water, a constant reminder of our watery evolution. Even today, our life begins swimming in our mother's watery womb and we come into the world in a rush of water. The water of the womb, called amniotic fluid, is actually the same density as sea water. No wonder I feel so held at home when I return to the sea.

The power of the sea to instantly bring me back to myself, to calm and restore, never ceases to amaze me. And yet, our desire to be cleansed, to wash away the stress and worries carried on land, has become tainted in an ocean that is fast becoming saturated with our human waste. My book *Ebb and Flow: Connect with the patterns and power of water*[2] was written as a response to our disconnect from the waters of our world. In the face of the multiple and unprecedented global crises we face, the loss of our emotional connection with the more-than-human world, especially 'wild water' in all its wonder and aliveness, is of deep concern.

Just pause to consider the vastness of the ocean for a moment – there is no part of the ocean that remains unaffected by the growing and interconnected pressures from climate change, biodiversity loss and further degradation caused by human activities and pollution. In turn, the impacts of the ocean (and marine environmental degradation) on human health are poorly considered. The most vivid example of how tangled our societal actions and human behaviour with water are is the emergence of plastic pollution in all the world's water bodies. Microplastics are so widespread that they are in our drinking water and entering our bodies, bloodstream and mother's breastmilk, with as yet poorly understood consequences.

We have lost our connection. If you have a deep connection with a particular place, it is likely that you might feel moved to do something.

You may even come to revere its sacredness. But if that deep connection is absent, how might we respond? For most of us, the water that sustains us every day remains 'out of sight, out of mind'. Modern society is designed to make us passive as we live in an 'always-on' culture with no time to reflect and give our attention to the world around us, let alone act. We feel socially isolated and are suffering an epidemic of loneliness, with the rise of mental health issues being one of the greatest crises of our time. Growing stress and anxiety are linked to the fact that we've become disconnected. We have lost the sense of deep connection with our aliveness with the natural world.

Water holds the answer. Water facilitates a full-bodied sense of connectedness with life. This is a central theme in my work as a blue health researcher (someone who researches the physical and mental health benefits of being close to or on water) and ocean advocate, how regular immersion and interaction with water can enhance this sense of connection, most especially activities like open-water swimming. This is linked to it being a highly immersive and multisensory activity, taking in the movement, colour, sounds, sensations and textures of water through all the body's senses. Going into the water and inhabiting our bodies fully is about being able to cross a threshold and enter into another world. It's a place where we can feel held by the water, where it is possible to express what we are feeling, to safely release whatever tension we are holding, all without judgement.

Restoring the health of the ocean and all water bodies will bring profound health benefits. Evidence shows that 'blue spaces', outdoor bodies of water, are among the most restorative environments for humans. Recent studies show how healthy coasts are associated with lower risk of depression, anxiety and other mental health disorders, as well as greater relaxation in adults and improved behavioural development and social connection in young people. Simply looking at the sea or listening to the sound of waves breaking has measurable benefits, calming our brain waves and soothing our frayed nervous systems.[3]

Like the flow of the water cycle, renewing our relationship with water is a cyclical tale of rhythm and movement, giving and receiving, inhalation and exhalation, ebb and flow, where water is at the beginning and end of every cycle of life.

Water acts as a powerful mirror – in it, we see ourselves and are reminded of our capacity to be like water; of our remarkable potential to recover and return to wholeness, to move fluidly and find flow and to embrace the unknown. Water teaches us the power of presence, the value of feeling and being with all of who we are so that we may act with greater clarity and empathy.

Indigenous water protectors and guardians like Diné (Navajo) and Lakota activist and ceremonial leader Pat McCabe and Mi'kmaq elder and Grassroots Grandmother Dorene Bernard have taught me much about our interrelationship with water, always reminding me that we belong to the water, we don't own it, and we are obliged to care for it.

So what can we learn from water and how can we bring our attention to the many ways we are mutually shaped and formed with and through our waterways and waterscapes?

Below are some practices that I hope will inspire you to form a relationship with your local living water systems and invite more presence and flow into your life. Make a commitment to your water to get to know it and listen to it, to cherish and protect it, and in turn to become known by the water and all that it gives life to. After all, our health and the health of this blue Earth depends on it.

1 **Journaling exercise – how well do you know your water?** Take a moment to reflect on where your nearest body of water is. Where is its source? For whom is this water home? How is this body of water doing? And as water scientist, legal scholar and citizen of the Shinnecock Nation Dr Kelsey Leonard reminds us to ask ourselves each day, 'What have I done for the water?'

2 **Connect with your ocean breath.** Bringing attention to my breath is one of the most direct and powerful ways for me to anchor myself in the present moment. It is a simple yet powerful way to connect with the ocean too, wherever you are. Every second breath we take comes from the ocean, from oxygen released by microscopic plants called phytoplankton. We are always connected with the ocean through our breath, which mirrors the ebb and flow of the tide. Slowing our breathing and extending our exhalation helps to calm our nervous system.

3 **Take a 'sound bath' and listen to the water.** The constant fullness and richness of water sounds, like the rhythmic pulse of breaking

waves, have a soothing effect on our brain. In an increasingly noisy world, water sounds are the antidote to the shrill staccato of traffic and other artificial sounds that create stress in the body. So every day take a few moments to tune into the natural sound bath of water.

4 **Look at water.** The sea is visually stimulating, with a thousand shades of constantly moving blue. According to clinical psychologist Richard Shuster, watching the sea alters the frequency of our brain waves, putting us in a more meditative state. So spend a few moments mindfully watching your local body of water ebb and flow.

5 **Honour your ebb.** Next time you find yourself near a body of water, take ten minutes to just sit and be still without focusing on anything. Let any thoughts or feelings that arise wash over you like a breaking wave and tune into all your senses while observing the water. If you find yourself getting distracted, just return to your breath. When the body and brain get a chance to rest and relax, our creative energy starts to flow.

Key action points for parents and providers of care

In many Indigenous cultures there is a belief that you need to allow time for your soul to catch up with your physical body, so it's important to take time to slow down, to pause and to rest – every day.

Paying more attention to my inner ebb and flow has made me more sensitive to life's imbalances and continues to teach me to live more in the moment so that I can be fully present with what is – rather than always going to the 'what if'. It's about trusting the process – which is less about trying to change things and more about choosing to be with the way things are.

Ultimately, it all comes back to the breath. Cold water stimulates the vagus nerve, which controls the parasympathetic nervous system (the fight-or-flight response) and connects the body and brain. Simply slowing the rate of breathing and extending every exhalation helps calm the nervous system and allows us to find a little ease in the everyday chaos. This simple practice is always available to us, so take some time every day to sit and breathe deeply (maybe inhale to a count of four, exhale slowing to a count of six), especially during difficult moments.

Note

1. Carson, Rachel, *Silent Spring*, new edn. Penguin Classics, 2000.
2. Britton, Easkey, *Ebb and Flow: Connect with the patterns and power of water.* Watkins, 2023.
3. Nichols, Wallace J., *Blue Mind*, 10th anniversary edition, Hachette, 2004.

13

Indigenous wisdom for troubled times

Tiokasin Ghosthorse

'This is the hardest time to live, but it is also the greatest honour to be alive now, and to be allowed to see this time. There is no other time like now. We should be thankful, for creation did not make weak spirits to live during this time. The old ones say "this is the time when the strongest spirits will live through and those who are empty shells, those who have lost the connection will not survive". We have become masters of survival – we will survive – it is our prophecy to do so.'

Tiokasin Ghosthorse

It is the popular mainstream belief that it takes a village to raise a child, but for me, as an Indigenous person, this phrase needs more coherent energy.

Firstly, let's explore the similarities and differences apparent int he fascinating world of Indigenous language. I'm eager to discuss which dichotomy best captures the essence of my protest, which is more than just a mere chant, but a powerful expression of knowing beyond the standardized and codified language of nouns. You will possibly read a different worldview, a non-worldly, non-imperialist approach, when trying to understand the meaning of clichéd language usage.

It is impossible to awaken someone who is pretending to be awake – in other words, the Western mind thinks it is in control but so often with the best of intentions misinterprets the more expressive Indigenous languages by standardizing everyone else's thinking to fit the traditional Western control.

I ride with a young, wild horse who understands, who understood before I became the nine-year-old upon its back, holding tightly to the life-giving mane. I couldn't saddle a horse single-handed at this young age, nor lift a saddle, to harness and summon up the strength to pull a cinch tightly enough to ensure that the oversized heavy leather that was invented to encumber any horse imbued with free movement was tightly in place.

Once on the four-legged wildness and purity, I shook and rubbed my face, my head and hair around his mane as he shook to feel who was on his back. And with an eye-to-eye glance, it was an instant communication of intuition that guided those few hours through the rolling hills. He would guide me alongside ravines where there were chokecherries, wild strawberries, black walnuts, sand berries, wild turnips, ground cherries and wild plums. I would eat all day and top it off with wild onions or scallions. In the middle of the hot summer days, the Missouri River flowing with Rocky Mountain sources provided fish and great swimming and playing.

I have always wanted to be older than I am, even when I was four. I didn't care about how much accumulated knowledge I would experience or how much I remembered. What mattered most to me was focusing on being conscious without being burdened by a conscience. And that led me to see differently as I sat on that hill on the prairie looking at the clouds at four summers young.

There I sat, pondering when the stars would appear as the sun cooled at the end of the day. I watched everything that crawled or slithered by me, flew by me, or walked by me. From the very beginning, I understood that Human Beings were not only defined by themselves but also by Earth and all her life forms, such as Stone, Water, Fire and Winds.

Today, I wonder what humans are doing to Human Beings by placing their 'human only' concept of humanity above all life forms – giving us a vague definition of humanity. And without empathy for Earth, there are very few *Human Beings* and too many *Human Doings* with illusionary saviour behaviours for humans only.

One cannot awaken someone pretending to be awake.

The educational institutions in the West offer an archaic and unrelatable teaching process that is disconnected from real life on Earth. It strips us of our heritage and forces us to 'utilize' reality instead of truly living with reality. The language used in the Western education curriculum rationalizes an inherently flawed philosophy of scarcity. The languages used are based on the Indo-European model, which is characterized by neediness, over-extraction and dependence, as if they are constantly seeking salvation and sustenance – the need to be perfect, the need to be correct and the need to prove.

It can be a challenge when attempting to articulate a written work that incorporates both hierarchical, linear narratives and the unexplainable nature of consciousness.

The compulsory education system in the West has drained the wisdom and knowledge from Indigenous minds. It has introduced foreign concepts that have no relation to the lands the system claims to have conquered. Despite this, Indigenous people who live in harmony with Earth encounter a Western paradigm that dismisses their thought processes. This has resulted in a systematic indoctrination that has led to the disappearance of cultures and the lands they were based on. To quote Albert Einstein, 'The intuitive mind is a sacred gift, and the rational mind is a faithful servant. We have created a society that honours the servant and has forgotten the gift.'

In 'Native Earth', extracted from *The Inner Journey: Views from native traditions*, Peter Matthiessen writes: 'In 1930, Albert Einstein visited a group of people who spoke the Uto-Aztecan language, which included the Hopi. He commented that among all peoples, 12-year-old children who spoke this language were probably the best equipped to understand his Theory of Relativity.' He continues:

> There seems no doubt that traditional peoples the world over have much to teach a spiritually-crippled race which, as Lame Deer said, sees 'only with one eye.' This half-blindedness has been the curse of the white people as long as the Indians have known us, but we have not always been accursed; at one time, we knew the *mysterium tremendum*. And we must feel awe again if we are to return to a harmonious existence with our own habitat and survive... When modern man has regained his respect for the Earth, when science has become a tool in the service of nature rather than a weapon to dominate it, then the lost Paradise, the Golden Age in the race memories of all people on Earth will come again, and all men will be "in Dios," People of God.[1]

Lakota have no word or concept for domination. We have understood that communication is not just gifted to Human Beings but that Beings have already used intelligence for millions, perhaps billions, of years before the recent entry of humans. We need to use a relating language, a relative language, when in relationship to all Beings, including Human Beings.

When we are born into this dimension, we are becoming Earth, and when we are living in this dimension, we are becoming Earth, and when we are leaving this dimension, we are becoming Earth. An at-once continuous relationship without ever having to use a 'connection' language because *we are becoming relationship to Earth*, the living relativity to Earth. Now, we must look to those very same Indigenous peoples who have been struggling to maintain living with reality rather than using reality.

Words bear meanings from ancient languages much older than the one I am using. Proper use of our Earthly tools is essential to create true magic. Illusions only lead to further disconnection from Mother Earth. *Magi* means one who makes magic by using the tools of Earth properly, such as a bird or fish using the wind and sun, while the fish uses the water properly. The magician, which the human has become with their use of technology, is fooling even themselves and thinking of being superior over those true *Magi*.

Respecting the power of words, not the concepts, the way Indigenous peoples do, by understanding the meaning of energy always in motion and not the stalemated definitions of nouns.

Lakota Wocekiye (prayer of thanks for acknowledging our interrelatedness)

I honor you in this circle of life with me. I am grateful for this opportunity to acknowledge you in this prayer. To The Creator, for the ultimate gift of life, I thank you.

To the Mineral Nation that has built & maintained my bones & all foundations of life experience, I thank you.

To the Plant Nation that sustains my organs, my body & gives me healing herbs for sickness, I thank you.

To the Animal Nation that feeds me from your own flesh & offers loyal companionship in this walk of life, I thank you.

To the Human Nation that shares my path as a soul upon the Sacred Wheel of earthly life, I thank you.

To the Spirit Nation that guides me invisibly through the ups & downs of life & for carrying the torch of light through Ages, I thank you.

To the Four Winds of Change & Growth, I thank you.

You are all my relations, my relatives, without whom I would not live.

We are in the circle of life together, co-existing, co-dependent, co-creating our destiny. One, no more important than the other.

One nation evolving from the other & yet each dependent upon the one above & the one below.

All of us a part of The Great Mystery.

Thank you for this Life.

Mitakuye Oyasin

Note

1. Matthiessen, Peter, 'Native Earth', in *The Inner Journey: Views from native traditions*, ed. Linda Hogan. Morning Light Press, 2009, pp. 128–43.

14

The whole being

Cornelius O'Shaughnessy

These are times of great change. As the old ways of being decay, we are birthing in a new world which is at once exciting yet terrifying. And whether we contract into fear or expand into wholeness depends on how well equipped we are to meet this moment as it comes. As adults we find this dance of fear and hope perplexing, but our children, our greatest hope for the future, are having to grow and mature midst this instability, while also finding the strength and resilience to meet the challenges of the world they have been born into. As adults and caregivers we need to ensure our children are given the tools they need to thrive, and if a solution to our current societal, political and environmental problems can be found, it will be found by them. With this in mind, it is our responsibility to ensure they have minds and hearts open and capable of meeting this moment. How we teach and guide them will define our future.

Currently, we are failing the younger generation. How much of their education is focused around teaching them how to become balanced and self-aware human beings who are harmoniously integrated with their environment and the people around them? We already know the answer. Now, more than ever, our children need to be met in a way that allows them to unleash the creativity, imagination, innovation and compassion that is within them and that the world so desperately needs. Living as we have been with an enormous wisdom deficit, we are paying the price in every area of our lives, most especially in the lives of our children who are not being taught how to feel into and live in their innate wholeness.

Through years of study and practice I have realized that many of the problems we are facing are born out of separation: separation from one another, from our communities, from our environment and separation from our own nature. We are merely existing disconnected from the flow of life. We do not spend enough time in nature. We are not taught to be intimately aware of the seasons and the ever-changing landscape around us, or to know where our food comes from and how to truly honour and care for our Mother Earth.

Being a 'good' human being, who is at one with their surroundings, is often seen as somewhat of an afterthought, an indulgence even, but when looking for the antidote to the madness around us, this is the missing piece. And having a better understanding of ourselves is as important as understanding those around us and our environment.

Who am I?

To me, reminding myself of this question is paramount to becoming a whole human being and living as I was born to do. Each one of us needs to ease off on the 'doing' so we can find a little space and stillness to truly understand who we are – our personality, our strengths and weaknesses and, if we are to find lasting happiness and inner peace, how we relate to our thoughts and emotions and who we are at the very deepest level of our being, the very foundation of our experience – our consciousness. It is our responsibility to first answer this question for ourselves before guiding our children towards a clearer and healthier understanding of themselves.

My story

My own story continues to be my greatest teacher. Growing up in a loving family in Maidenhead, UK, I was a happy child, always fascinated by nature and spirituality, but was told time and time again that neither would equip me for the world I was living in. Sadly, no amount of maths, physics, business studies or chemistry helped me navigate the challenges I faced during my younger years and it was only in retrospect that I learned that the environment and the world I grew up in was too harsh for my sensitive soul.

At the age of 14, due to a combination of my parents' separation and financial struggles, I started to experience severe anxiety and depression. My sense of stability and safety had disappeared. Spending time with a rowdy group of teenagers, I experimented with drugs and discovered another world I could easily escape to. At 17, I met someone who I believed would become my soulmate, but that swiftly became a toxic relationship that continued for five years. The following few years were among my most challenging. The only world I knew shattered to pieces around me, leading to mental collapse and constant thoughts of suicide. I had lived through what I now know is post-traumatic stress disorder, or PTSD while also suffering with undiagnosed Lyme disease and a nerve disorder. I tried numerous antidepressant medications and therapies but was told by my doctor that I was 'treatment resistant'. The faint glimpses of mental stability I happened upon generally lasted a few days before the deep, dark sadness and depression returned. I tried numerous herbs, acupuncture, homeopathy, but living as I was in a constant state of anxiety and stress, it proved difficult for any meaningful benefit to take hold.

Carrying this pain, I began my spiritual search, breaking away from the bounds of my Catholic faith and visiting lamas, gurus, priests, saints and sages from all paths and walks of life. I spent long periods of time studying with New Age gurus and experimenting with crystals and myriad practices – a combination of which did lend some stability to my unhinged inner world – but they did not delve deeply enough into the layers of my prolonged sadness and grief.

I was introduced to meditation at 15 by Palgyi, a Buddhist monk who visited my home town. Sitting together, he asked me to simply focus on my breath. With every in breath he said, 'Now light is coming into your mind,' and with each outbreath, 'Now darkness is leaving you.' I soon realized that this simple practice was a warm place where I could find refuge and peace, at least for a short time. My mind was unsettled, so sitting still was difficult, but sometimes I walked while focusing on my breath and this helped too. These were the first beautiful steps on my never-ending journey of exploration with the Eastern perspective.

During my twenties, I became increasingly fixated on Buddhism's promise of freedom from suffering and the wisdom of many of the profound teachers of India. I continued to read, study and meditate, all the while moving deeper and closer into the exploration of my mind and my life. With this came further moments of ease and clarity. Yet I still could not find peace.

I had been going back and forth to India, enthralled by its charming, seductive chaos that, as soon as you land, entices you on a journey of discovery. During one of my many visits, I found myself in the ancient village of Hampi in Karnataka, a quiet, spiritual place with temples, monkeys and mystery everywhere – just as one imagines India to be. It was incredibly hot. After settling into the daily Hampi flow – walking, sitting, eating, sleeping and not a lot else – a growing sense of surrender slowly began to ripen in my soul.

One afternoon as I sat in the hot haze looking over the rice fields, the food of life for most Indian people, I was overcome with a real feeling of acceptance for myself, for my suffering, for where I was at in my life and for the greater world. Gazing out, I realized that life was doing what life was doing and I was a mere speck of dust screaming about it. So I just let go of the feeling that anything needed to change. I stopped resisting. I surrendered. I realized that until that moment my relationship with life was transactional, as I was always selfishly asking for what I didn't have and resisting what I did. This surrender wasn't a desperate and hopeless throwing in of the towel. Far from it actually, as it was infused with a sense of quiet finality. I had been searching for a cure for my mind, for my back, for my digestive issues, and I had been seeking peace, seeking God and seeking freedom from suffering, but all I found was just enough wisdom to occasionally enter the eye of the storm, before withdrawing again. By accepting my problems as they were, I started to show up with less desire and more peace and my pain began to release. And the irony is that when you stop trying to fix it – it gets a little better!

My life lit up as if everything around and in me was flowing again after years of stagnation. I was still in physical pain, my life was still a mess, but day by day I was deepening into resolute peace. Every person, place and moment was a teacher, leading me deeper and closer to my true self. My brain felt as though it was on fire, as wisdom rose up to meet my sadness, tears flowed and the knots of anxiety and depression lifted. It was as if I had been asleep in another world for years, as the clouds of despair lifted and I awoke to this world. An unshakeable clarity about myself and my life permeated my being and I knew then that regardless of how much pain or joy I felt, this clarity would not disappear. I realized that what broke my heart also opened by heart and that with patience and stillness, the light in my life would emerge from the darkness.

Now in my forties, my life continues to overflow with challenges and periods of sadness and grief. However, in among the turmoil, I have an inner knowing and strength that guides and sustains me.

I see life, myself and others differently now – I had tried so hard to wish my suffering away, but in the end my suffering was the thick, dark mud from which the lotus arose. My years of pain had not only led me on a journey towards enlightenment, but they had also caused an alchemical reaction that fully awakened me. While I use the word 'me', what I realize is that there is no 'me'. There is only the dance of life and I along with everyone else and everything around us are that dance. We are one collective being. The further I move along my journey, the more I perceive the subtleties, paradoxes that at the time were beyond the ability of my intellect to grasp or explain.

I am still painfully human, with weakness, failings and suffering, but as time goes on, I see all of this as a beautifully expanded vision of wholeness. I think at times I may even suffer more now because the world seems to break my heart more than it ever did before, but my suffering feels very different, meaningful even. My suffering is more of a yearning for the divine, perhaps even a prayer that can lead myself and others to greater happiness and freedom.

I do understand the problems people, both young and older, are living through today, and I try to help them realize that there is a way to meet these issues differently. I owe everything to the rich and wise paths of Buddhism, Advaita Vedanta, Sufism and Christianity and continue to drink wisdom from these teachings, and the fruit that comes from following them. There is wisdom and love in all paths to the divine. There has to be, as this is the only way to reach God, Brahman, Christ, the Buddha Nature – whatever name you wish to give it.

I have come to see the mystical heart in many paths, and I have learned that I don't need to convert anyone to anything. Instead, I meet people where they are at and help them realize how their own path and its teachings can help them to live a happier and better life.

With these ever-rolling emergencies in our world, our immediate reaction comes from a state of panic and fear, which creates an unsafe space within. Through my experience and teachings I help people rise and respond to this chaos in a wiser, more compassionate way. I don't try to fix anything, but by becoming a mirror to what's going on within and around them, I help people see themselves and life more clearly. And once they surrender to what is, those unhealthy patterns naturally start to break. With guidance, the seeds of acceptance, surrender and wisdom and a genuine interest in others' wellbeing will start to bloom.

I seek to challenge, debase and undermine views that are extreme, intolerant or unkind, sometimes by directly confronting the views of others, while other times quietly stretching out these views to their natural conclusion and helping people better understand where their negative thinking may lead them. However, regardless of the method, the fruit of the teachings is the wisdom and love that spring to life naturally once we invite them in and give them the space they need to grow. The most important message I give to all my students, young or old, is to be in a state of selfless service.

What I have learned

I have spent many years dissecting my experiences, the wisdom I have encountered, and how my seemingly never-ending tunnel of darkness turned into clarity, confidence and a lasting sense of wholeness. My job now, my commitment, purpose and practice, is to create the conditions where wisdom and loving kindness can flourish so others can take that first step on their unique journey to love and wholeness too, regardless of their stage in life.

The past years have taught me a lot, much of it learned the hard way. But do I regret it? Absolutely *not* – as it led me to where I am now. It taught me that life really is a mess and that's how it is supposed to be! And while we can't always control what happens to us, we can work with our reaction to what is happening, so we can better meet these experiences, emotions and thoughts as they arise.

I learned that suffering incubates transformation in a way that happiness never could, and while we do not choose to suffer, when it chooses us, it comes with a gift, a secret hidden wisdom. Once we choose to meet our suffering, and that of the world, with love and wisdom using the practices outlined below, a profound transformation of the heart and mind is certain.

Through many years of practising meditation I now help others realize that the real art of meditation lies in doing nothing, just sitting with the mess in your mind, without trying to fix it. There is nothing wrong with this mess – it's the layers of resistance we build up around us that create the problems. Our inner and outer turmoil may feel like poison to us, but it is also the soil from which the antidote arises.

I know that thoughts and emotions are an important part of the human experience. They help us navigate life, but they are not who we are. They are conditioned responses and reactions. We witness them, watching and experiencing them as they come and go. Through careful observation we come to see that we are the consciousness by which our thoughts and emotions are known. If we look at our direct experience, we can see that they come and go and that we, simply being aware of them, are not coming and going. Our awareness is always there, shining, resplendent, a constant in the sea of changing thoughts, emotions and perceptions.

Once we sit quietly and become the silent witness watching these thoughts and emotions coming and going, like the waves on the shore, we can begin to see beyond them, to the ever-present awareness within us. We come to know ourselves better and uncover a more stable and peaceful mind. And we discover our true nature.

I have learned that:
- Suffering causes transformation and that it is an essential component of change. It is the mud from which the lotus arises. The lotus is beautiful, but it is the mud that gives it the nutrients needed to burst into the light with glorious flowers. No mud, no lotus.
- We all have the capacity to flourish in ways we would not believe possible. It is the very act of us descending into our own darkness and suffering that causes us to reach for the light and transform into a brighter and better human.

I have learned that acceptance, surrender, wisdom and kindness are essential to being fully embodied human beings. I have learned to sit and to just *be* still more – the more I do this, the better everything becomes.

I now know that knowing ourselves and creating inner peace are the most powerful gifts we can give to the world and pass on to our children and others in our care. If we can help them to find deeper meaning and a way to rise and meet the challenges they face, then we can use this moment in history to ignite a renaissance. It is only wisdom that will allow us to take the madness we have before us and skilfully use it to birth an entirely new way of being for all of us and for the Earth.

Always remember...

The birth of anything new is not easy. The rapid changes we are experiencing in our lives and the chaos unfolding around us are the labour pains of a new way of being. We are in crisis, but we are also just moments away from an explosion in human potential. As parents, teachers and providers of care for young people, we must equip the next generation with the wisdom and compassion needed to meet this moment. It takes time and practice. These teachings and practices are the way back to wholeness.

Don't always look at the darkness in your experience, look instead to see what grows from it – just as the lotus rises from the mud. These 5,000-plus-year-old-teachings are not a luxury, they are a birthright, and my wish is that this wisdom will teach us all, young and older, to dance in the fire.

Simple practices for becoming whole

The following time-tested practices are the simple foundations that will bring the wisdom we are seeking into being. Practised regularly, they can help us all, parents, providers of care for young people, and teenagers and young adults themselves, to live happier and more wholesome lives. The sooner we begin to practise these ourselves and the earlier we pass them on to the next generation, the more equipped they will be to face the challenges of this new world we call home. Some of these exercises are perfect for the classroom setting, too, as just a few moments of stillness in the school day can make a big difference, every day. While there is no perfect time of day to practise, many people find that early morning works best, before the day begins, or before the school day begins in the classroom. But remember, the ideal time is the time that works best for you.

Often, our suffering is caused by us getting 'stuck' in our heads, in our thoughts and emotions. Thoughts and feelings are not our reality unless we make them so by bringing them to life. Practices like this give us space away from the clutter in our minds to open us up to an easier and freer way of living. At the same time they allow us to relate to our thoughts and feelings in a more positive, natural and harmonious way.

Remember, we are all different. When working with young people, see where each student is at before guiding them towards those practices that may work best for them. When starting out, it is advisable to work with an experienced meditation teacher who understands these practices and knows which are most suited to each individual. For some, simply spending time in nature may be the most appropriate practice.

Simple sitting meditation practice
1–20 minutes

Perhaps the easiest and most effective way to find a little peace, stability and mental strength in your day is to develop a simple meditation practice. We know that meditation helps us navigate life in a wiser, more centred and compassionate way by training the mind to discover moments of calm and stillness in the storm of the endless thoughts and emotions. It is never too late to start your meditation journey – remember, the earlier you start, the better. Once a few moments of daily meditation becomes habit then it becomes an accessible place of refuge to drop into anytime and anywhere. This simple practice shows us how we can all self-regulate and find inner freedom even during the most challenging circumstances.

The practice

- Sit in a comfortable but upright position, either cross-legged on the floor or on a cushion or upright on a chair. If sitting on a chair, use a straight-backed chair and allow your feet to be flat on the floor, with legs uncrossed. Sit with grace and dignity so your posture can mirror how you would like to meet the world.
- Soften, open and relax your shoulders and find a little softness in your face and jaws too.
- Gently close your eyes if it feels comfortable or lower your gaze. If your eyes remain open, allow your gaze to settle gently on some nearby object.

- Breathe naturally in and out through your nose.
- Bring attention to your nose, the inside of your nose, and fix your attention there.
- Feel the sensation of the air as it moves in and out through your nostrils. Continue breathing and sensing the sensations.
- Distraction is normal, even during a very short practice. This is part of the process, so do not view it as an obstacle to finding ease. When you realize your attention has strayed, simply bring it back to your breath, every time. It's here that we often have thoughts like 'I can't do this', 'I can't meditate', but it is the endless distractions and us meeting them by returning the focus to our breath that trains the mind. This is meditation.
- Some people find it helpful to silently recite a word or short phrase in accordance with their breath. If so, silently recite the sound '*SO*' with each in breath and '*HUM*' with the out breath. If we listen carefully, this is what the breath actually sounds like. Many young people in particular find this can make the practice easier.
- When the practice is finished, just sit for a few more breaths before getting on with your day.

Begin by sitting like this in stillness and ease for just 1 minute every day for one week. The following week increase your time to 2 minutes, then 3 minutes the week after that... building up week by week to 5 minutes, then 10, then 15, then 20 minutes – and longer if you would like.

Many people find that 20 minutes is the ideal time for regular practice. If you are over 16 years old and are comfortable with longer time periods, continue to build your time using 5-minute intervals up to 40 minutes. To avoid continually checking the time on a clock or phone, especially as you increase the length of time you are sitting, just set an alarm (many apps have timers with a simple bell or chime). Don't use a waking alarm as it's too jolting. Others may find that 3 minutes a day is enough. If that is you, then as long as you find the time to meditate every day, that is what makes the difference. Remember, it is not the length of time that matters, most especially at a young age, but anchoring the practice into your day, every day. You will soon feel the benefits and you will want to continue.

Teaching prompts when helping children and young adults learning a meditation practice of their own

- Remind them that it can be boring and that is okay! This is not about excitement or about the practice being entertaining – that is not the point. In truth, we want to let the mind get bored. We are training the mind and reaping the long-term benefits.
- Distraction is welcome and to be accepted. People often think they aren't meditating correctly if they get distracted, but it's normal too. This is how we train the mind. It doesn't matter how long you've been distracted or what you are distracted by, as soon as you can, just return to the breath and to the practice.
- Young people in particular may find the word 'meditation' a challenge. If so, using 'stillness' or 'sitting in stillness' may prove more acceptable and doable.

Being present practice

15–20 minutes

While there are myriad definitions of the word 'mindfulness', to me it can be summed up as simply being aware of what is happening around us. We do this by letting go of our internal chatter and bringing our attention to what is happening in the present moment. This can be done with eyes open or closed. The following practice incorporates both.

- Sitting comfortably upright with your eyes closed, use the simple sitting meditation practice (above) to bring some calm and ease into your body and mind for a few minutes. Then, keeping your eyes closed, stop focusing on your breath and become aware of your thoughts and feelings and any sounds or sensations. Be present with them all.
- Just like in the simple sitting meditation, when your mind wanders (as it inevitably will), bring your attention back to what is happening at this moment. Let go of any judgements and assessments about what is happening and simply *be* with what is arising. Remain like this for approximately 10 minutes.
- Now open your eyes and repeat the same practice for a further 3 minutes.

A simple exercise in acceptance
15–20 minutes

Many of us move through the world chasing what we want and avoiding what we don't. This is perfectly normal and to be encouraged as it is important to have a clear idea of what career we might want to strive for, the journeys we wish to experience or the partner we wish to have in life, and so on. But when we apply it to myriad things in an obsessive way, it can become problematic, creating a stressful internal environment. We are all guilty of this to some degree. Surrender and acceptance are the antidote.

We will arrive here naturally through meditation and being present, but this exercise will help us deepen more quickly. This practice is not about accepting everything in life without boundaries or action to change certain things. Instead, we are learning how to avoid becoming absorbed and tormented by the endless, unhelpful and destructive tendencies of the mind, be it to obsessively praise or condemn, or feverishly trying to avoid what we have to experience or endure, all of which creates an unhealthy way of being with ourselves and a mind that is unstable and obsessively seeking pleasure.

Here's how

- Sit and practise a few minutes of meditation (as above), followed by a few minutes of being present (as above), then with your eyes closed, allow yourself to accept all that arises. As thoughts, sounds, sensations and emotions arise, your mind will naturally embrace some aspects of the experience, but reject other parts. With this acceptance technique we simply remove the value from these judgements and assessments by accepting *all* that arises. We simply sit with what is and accept it all.
- Then we can move a little deeper still by accepting our humanness, our weaknesses, the positive and negative experiences we have had, the people in our lives and the world around us. Accept it all as part of the messy and untamed experience that is life. Once we accept it all, we can start to release certain feelings and emotions that have been holding us back and move on with greater ease. In essence, with acceptance we can start to soften and open up to a new way of being.

Practice for generating compassion
10–15 minutes

This practice is powerful. It helps bring love into being. By giving love to others, we become kinder, more loving beings, better able to give and accept love from others.

- Follow each of the meditation, mindfulness and acceptance practices above for about 5–6 minutes.
- Now bring your attention to your thought, emotions and your own body and send them loving kindness. Now bring your attention to someone that you love and send them love. Then hold your family in your mind and send them love. Then hold your friends in your mind and send them love. Then hold your enemies in mind and send them love. Then your community, your workplace or school. Send them all love. Then your country, the Earth, this solar system and the universe – send love.
- This should take about a further 10–15 minutes. After doing so, pause before moving on with your day.

This practice helps expand our circle of love and compassion and train the mind to meet others and to meet everything, including the challenging people and circumstances in our life, with love.

Follow-up questions when working with young people
- What are the obstacles to love and how can we overcome these obstacles?
- How does love help us all to live better and more wholesome lives?
- How can we act on this love?
- How can we bring this love into being?

Noticing consciousness
20 minutes+, suitable for 16 years and older

This practice is a step deeper than the last. Start with the previous steps for 5 minutes.

While not easy, this exercise is very powerful and when performed regularly allows us to see ourselves beyond our conditioned thoughts, perceptions and beliefs.

The fact that we are conscious beings is the most significant and most overlooked part of our experience. We can all too easily identify with thoughts and emotions, constructing our sense of who we are from them. But thoughts and emotions come and go. Consciousness is there all the time. It is the very root of our being. If we are anything, we are consciousness, more than we are thought and emotion.

We are used to looking at and being aware of objects, thoughts and emotions and experiences, but we never look at the consciousness by which all these things are known. It is consciousness that allows us to be aware and to perceive the world.

Many of the ancient teachings suggest that the consciousness we are experiencing is the very field of being from which everything arises and to which everything returns, and more recently many scientists have started to explore this. To the ancients, our ego is an illusion and our true nature is consciousness; some traditions may call this the soul. The real beauty of the method of spiritual enquiry (unlike the Western scientific method) is that we don't need answers to this question – instead we look and see what we can discover for ourselves.

This following exercise is designed to help us deepen our awareness of consciousness, but it can take some time to become confident and comfortable with the practice.

Here's how

- Settle yourself for several minutes doing the practices above (5–10 minutes each, depending on the time available). Then simply bring your awareness to the fact that you are aware. Some people can find this tricky as we are conditioned to look at thoughts and emotions arising before us but not turning the mind inwards and looking at the consciousness by which these thoughts and emotions are known.
- If you are finding it difficult to be aware of being aware, just ask yourself, 'To whom is this experience arising?' or 'Who am I?' Don't look for an intellectual answer to this question; instead look into your direct experience. You will find the answer here.

In other words, look at yourself: who am I? Notice that thoughts come and go, but you are not coming and going. What is it that is not coming and going? Look there. This can be challenging at first because we are not used to looking at ourselves this deeply, but bear with it. In time you will discover that our thoughts and emotions are simply clouds passing by and that our true nature is the vast open sky of clear consciousness in which they are moving.

Seeing this helps ease the mind from the cacophony of thoughts and emotions that we experience each day. They may not disappear, but the more we practise, the more we will notice that we don't cling on to these thoughts and emotions, they don't define us, and it becomes easier and more natural to let go and be still, happy and more at ease.

With this practice you simply notice that you are aware and stay with this noticing of awareness - be aware of being aware. Stay with your awareness of being aware.

Prayer

Prayer is a yearning from the heart for growth and renewal and it helps guide the awakening process. To begin with it is simply recognizing our weaknesses, suffering, the suffering of the world, and our inability to overcome all of this. We surrender to it all, to life/God/reality and ask for help. ask life/God/reality for mercy, guidance, salvation and renewal.

'Be still and know that I am God.' As our prayer evolves, we find that our time in prayer starts to become more and more silent, we ask for less and less, instead resting in stillness.

Prayer is a conversation between ourselves and Life, God, the Buddha, nature, the Universe, the Divine Mother, nature, whichever words or beliefs resonate best. It is not our ideas or beliefs that are important, it is our openness and humility, the quality of our heart and mind as we open up to the Infinite. Once we know that life is alive and ready to meet us, regardless of our religious beliefs, as long as our heart is pure and centered in love, in does.

Being in nature
Do this every day for as long as you can

It continues to amaze me how many people struggle to find some connection with the natural world around them, as though it is an impossible task or one that requires skilful practices or hidden techniques. But those who spend time in nature know how easy it is. You just have to spend time in nature while being quiet and still yourself. For some, it may be gardening or bird watching; for others, it's walking, running or hiking in nature.

The above practices can all be carried out in nature. Just walking and paying attention to the surroundings, the leaves and trees, the wind, the clouds, the colours and sounds is being present with nature. Let nature be seen and heard – let it permeate every cell of your being.

Follow-up questions when working with others

Ask your child/student/client to think about the following questions for a few moments after every practice, especially when they are new to meditation:

- How was this practice?
- How does this practice make you feel?
- How might this practice help you in your life?
- How might you integrate this into your day?

There is no wrong way to do these exercises. The real beauty is that by simply continuing to practise them, we come to a deeper experience of them. Always reassure students that they are doing the practice right and that everything they are feeling and experiencing is part of the practice – and that simply doing it repeatedly is what matters. With guidance and ongoing support, the student will naturally refine their own practice. While some will find boredom to be an obstacle, others may complain of distraction – regardless of the complaint, remind them to come back to their practice, always. With time and ongoing gentle guidance, everything will resolve itself.

15

Nourishing body and mind

Charlotte Fraser

'The White Rabbit put on his spectacles. "Where shall I begin, please your Majesty?" he asked. "Begin at the beginning," the King said gravely, "and go on till you come to the end: then stop."'

Lewis Carroll, *Alice in Wonderland*

Headaches, acne, cramps and body odour, and being tired on waking, mood swings and anxiety, are often considered typical teenage traits. As a naturopathic nutritionist I always view these symptoms through a different lens, as to me they are all signs and symptoms of compromised physical, mental and emotional health. After all, this is our body's only means of communicating, so how else is it to express an unmet need, one frequently associated with a 'nutrition gap'? In the case of certain young people, such as those who self-harm, their body might also be their only means of expression or it may feel that way to them.

Addressing deficiencies and imbalances in vitamins, minerals and gut microbes can make a profound difference to a young person's physical, emotional and mental wellbeing. Now, as scientific cognitive testing also attests, correcting nutritional imbalances can significantly improve cognition, memory, attention and reasoning skills, and verbal ability. Furthermore, a holistic approach to each young person holds the potential to deliver lasting health benefits, as many of the chronic health issues observed in my adult nutrition clients take root around puberty.

A significant aspect of my nutrition work revolves around communication. This encompasses interpreting the body's signs and symptoms and, most importantly, empowering clients to become their own experts by enabling them to better decipher and comprehend the myriad signs and symptoms that manifest in their bodies. There really is a world of difference between being 'body conscious', as many teenagers are, and being able to connect, appreciate and wholly embody our body so we can all 'feel good in our skin'. This also involves optimizing our body's intricate internal metabolic and microbial signalling pathways – by, for example, eating fewer refined sugars and highly processed foods which can contribute to insulin resistance and metabolic dysfunction, or integrating intermittent fasting and eating prebiotic-rich foods to nourish our good bacteria. Maintaining a healthy weight through a combination of a colourful, nutritiously diverse and balanced diet, regular physical activity, adequate sleep and down time can help reduce excess body weight, especially abdominal fat, which is associated with serious metabolic issues.

The gut–brain axis

The gut–brain axis, and the close association between what and how we eat and our gut and mental and emotional health, is now well documented and has become one of the most interesting and emerging areas of current scientific research.

Akin to a biological fingerprint or signature, every gut microbiome is unique. It is the embodiment of all our individual genetic, physical, mental, emotional, environmental, social and cultural experiences. Our DNA initially shapes our microbiota, with our first exposure to microorganisms occurring during childbirth in the birth canal and through our mother's breast milk, if we were breastfed. As we grow, environmental factors, dietary choices and lifestyle can either nurture a microbiome and support good health or predispose us to greater risk of disease. Numerous factors influence this 'nutrient bank balance', including genetics, age, diet, lifestyle, underlying health conditions, exposure to antibiotics and other medications, as well as environmental, cultural and social factors.

The nutritional bank balance of our bodies is dependent on the following key factors, and a shortfall in any of these elements creates a nutrition gap, which can potentially adversely affect immediate and long-term health:

- individual food choices
- food growing, processing and preparation methods
- the nutrient content of the food we eat
- the ability of the body to assimilate these nutrients
- lifestyle factors, such as quality of sleep, stress, smoking, vaping, alcohol intake, drugs, birth control and medications

- activity levels and energy expenditure
- over-supplementation in certain vitamins and minerals, which can disrupt overall balance.

While some individuals start life with a rich balance of microbes, vitamins and minerals, others have nutritional deficiencies from birth. The good news is that by adopting a holistic nutritional approach as early as possible in life, we can replenish our nutrient bank balance for optimal health.

Eating a diverse diet is key to ensuring our body gets this wide range of essential nutrients. This includes eating a variety of fruits, vegetables, whole grains, lean proteins, fermented foods and healthy fats. Different foods contain different nutrients, so mixing foods helps ensure our body gets what it needs. Eating a variety of plants and incorporating probiotic and prebiotic foods (see the list of recommended foods in the Appendix) is also key to optimizing our gut microbiome. Numerous studies now support how these essential bacteria strengthen our immune system (70 per cent of which is located in our gut) and yield far-reaching benefits for our overall physical, cognitive, mental and emotional health. While individually miniscule, these microbes collectively yield immense power, much like an elephant, shaping various aspects of our health and wellbeing. In this context, it's also used metaphorically to emphasize the substantial impact that our body's microbial composition has on our health and wellbeing, despite it being frequently overlooked or considered too controversial or inconvenient. The rise in obesity, anxiety and depression among teenagers is a monumental, elephant-sized problem.[1]

This said, microbial statistics are constantly being challenged as newly identified microbes come to the fore. For example, 4,993 previously unknown microbes have recently been identified by ZOE, the company co-founded by Tim Spector, professor of genetic epidemiology at King's College London. Many of these have yet to be named.

Common dietary mistakes

Through my many years of working, one of the biggest issues I have continued to see is the elimination of entire food groups from clients' daily diets. As a result they are missing out on all the associated phytonutrients and anti-inflammatory, health-promoting microbes that are present in these food groups.

- Eliminating all dairy products reduces exposure to valuable sources of beneficial microbes. Cow's milk and yoghurt are two of nature's best sources of iodine. *Lactobacillus rhamnosus** and *Limosilactobacillus reuteri* (or *L. reuteri*)** are currently being researched as potential psychobiotics beneficial for reducing anxiety.
- Eliminating all animal produce can lead to deficiencies in essential nutrients such as vitamin B_{12}, iron and zinc.
- Choosing a gluten-free diet is very common among young people. While it can be a healthy and advisable way of eating for some, it often results in the exclusion of whole grains, an important source of fibre, as well as a deficiency in B vitamins and magnesium. Both the B group of vitamins and magnesium are essential for helping to reduce anxiety and stress.
- Eliminating carbohydrates from the daily diet impacts the beneficial butyrate-producing bacteria. These essential bacteria feed on insoluble fibre and resistant starch and play important roles in balancing other bacterial levels, while also maintaining the body's mucosal barrier, modulating the immune host response, preventing infections and regulating energy expenditure.
- Excluding random foods because of a suspected food intolerance and not compensating for the nutrient and microbial loss can result in nutritional deficiencies that may impact physical, emotional and mental health.

I have also noticed that many of my vegetarian clients are consuming fewer vegetables than their meat-eating counterparts. Their diets tend to be higher in fruits and carbohydrates in general, with the cheese and tomato baguette serving as a good example. Similarly, it is widely believed that few foods actually survive our stomach acid to reach

---

* Sources of *L. rhamnosus* include bio yogurt, kefir, and other fermented dairy products, some cheeses (e.g. Parmigiano Reggiano and Gruyère), kimchi, sauerkraut, tempeh and miso.

** Sources of *L. reuteri* include beastmilk, some fermented dairy products like kefir and bio yoghurt, some 'probiotic' cheeses such as aged Cheddar, Grana Padano, Gruyère and Parmigiano Reggiano, also unpasteurized sauerkraut and kimchi. *L. reuteri* is not easily found in high street brands of kefir or yoghurt; check the product website or, safer still, make your own.

our gut microbes in the first place and that many of the 'foods' we consume daily are so ultra-processed that they are beyond nutritional recognition.

Is it any wonder, then, that some of our friendly essential microbes are missing?

Puberty

Puberty is akin to a biological earthquake. Nutritional fault lines come to the surface more prominently during these critical growing years for several reasons:

- **Increased nutrient requirements:** puberty is a period of rapid growth and development with significant physical and hormonal changes. The body needs higher levels of nutrients such as protein for muscle growth, calcium for bone development and iron for blood production, also zinc for myriad reasons outlined below. If a growing child's diet doesn't meet these increased nutritional demands, deficiencies can and are likely to occur.
- **Growth spurts:** rapid growth during puberty places additional strain on the body's nutritional resources.
- **Dietary changes:** many adolescents change their eating habits and dietary choices during these years as they become more independent in their food choices and more influenced by peers (rather than parents), leading to potential imbalances and deficiencies. This can be exacerbated by a preference for ultra-processed and fast foods that are often low in essential nutrients.
- **Poor eating habits:** adolescents and young adults often skip meals, eat irregularly or engage in fad and restricted diets. Peer pressure, body image concerns, social media trends and societal influences also contribute to unhealthy eating habits.
- **Dehydration:** this is a common problem with adolescents. Water consumption should be evaluated in relation to overall sugar intake, physical activity and stress levels within any given day. Constipation, diarrhoea, bloating, headaches, panic attacks and cramps can all be associated with chronic dehydration, with increased histamine levels triggering the body's inflammatory process.

- **Poor nutrient absorption:** some health conditions affect nutrient absorption, for example coeliac disease and inflammatory bowel disease.
- **Increased physical activity:** during puberty many adolescents become more physically active, engaging in sports and other activities that will increase their energy and nutrient requirements. Additionally, a significant number of them experience inadequate sleep – sleep is crucial for effective recovery and repair.

Common fault lines

Trinity of gut health
Zinc–iron–copper balance: key to immune, gut, hormonal, skin, thyroid, cognitive and mental health

In my experience many health issues start here. One of the most common fault lines to emerge during puberty pivots around internal zinc–iron–copper balance, or what I refer to as the 'trinity of gut health'.

Many people tend to look at everything in isolation and each nutrient individually rather than considering the whole food and the needs of the body as a dynamic whole. This is a big problem that continues to impact our collective health and wellbeing.

Please note, I often refer to zinc as the 'gut mineral' because of its pivotal role in upholding the integrity of the mucous membrane that lines the gastrointestinal tract. However, I refer to the trinity of zinc, copper and iron because these minerals all compete for the same absorption sites in the body and must be kept in balance; excessive intake of one can interfere with the absorption or utilization of the others. Deficiencies and imbalances in these key minerals are implicated in many of the gut and cognitive health problems prevalent today, including autoimmune diseases, hormonal imbalances, thyroid problems, mental health issues and eating disorders.

Zinc is a constituent of more than 2,000 enzymes that play crucial roles in digestion and metabolism in the body. It is essential for the production and regulation of thyroid hormones, sex hormones (testosterone and oestrogen), adrenal hormones, growth hormone, immune system hormones, and the synthesis, storage and secretion of insulin.

Some children are born with low levels of zinc, but it is only during the tectonic shifts of puberty that these problems begin to surface as the body needs more zinc to support rapid growth and hormonal activity. Zinc plays a crucial role in hormone production and regulation within the body and a deficiency can trigger a domino effect, contributing to gut dysbiosis (imbalance), poor iron absorption, poor vitamin B and protein synthesis and blood sugar imbalances.

Animal studies have demonstrated that zinc deficiency can lead to stunted growth, delayed sexual maturation, compromised immunity and profound pathological alterations in the body.[2] Zinc is essential for the body's internal switchboard and coding, as well as gene expression (whether we activate or suppress a particular gene). It also contributes to DNA replication, transcription, protein synthesis and cell growth.

Neither animals nor microbes possess the innate ability to synthesize zinc, and this makes their ability to manage and use zinc pivotal for their survival and development. Typically, animals and microbes can self-regulate their internal zinc concentration to maintain normal metabolic functions. However, too much zinc can be harmful to the cells in the body, while any deficiency disrupts important internal processes, including the transmission of signals between cells.

An imbalance in zinc and copper levels in the body can be implicated in iron-deficiency anaemia. Both zinc and copper aid iron absorption, and while iron supplements are routinely prescribed when iron deficiency shows up in a blood test, individual zinc and copper levels are rarely, if ever, considered. However, supplementing iron alone can further deplete zinc and copper levels, thereby perpetuating a vicious circle.

Demand for iron also increases during periods of rapid growth in the body. Iron is essential for supporting growth and development and for haemoglobin production, stress and disease resistance and the metabolism of the B group of vitamins. Iron-deficiency anaemia is common during puberty, especially in girls due to menstrual blood loss, and as with zinc deficiency, it is more prevalent among vegetarians, vegans and restrictive dieters.

Copper deficiency is relatively rare as most people get an adequate amount through their diet. Certain medical conditions or dietary factors can contribute to copper deficiency. These include celiac disease, Crohn's disease and other gastrointestinal idsorders that may impair copper absorption, as well as high iron intake and/or excessive zinc supplementation over an extended period of time. Copper is an essential trace element, vital for various bodily functions, including the formation of haemoglobin for oxygen transport in red blood cells, as well as immune health, skin and hair pigmentation and bone health. Copper also plays a role in the synthesis of certain B vitamins, particularly vitamin B_{12}, which is a common deficiency among long-term vegetarians and vegans especially.

- *Signs and symptoms relating to zinc imbalance:* premature birth, infant colic, slow growth, late onset of puberty, eczema, skin rashes, asthma, allergies, food intolerances, fatigue, hay fever, acne, warts, mouth ulcers, frequent colds and flu, tonsilitis, sinusitis, white spots on nails, constipation, diarrhoea, bloating, heartburn, OCD (Obsessive Compulsive Disorder), perfectionism (anxiety), poor memory, poor verbal reasoning, infrequent/cessation of periods, hair loss, bottling emotion, ruminating over the past, grief, depression, poor sense of taste or smell, poor wound healing, loss of appetite, addiction, anorexia and self-harm.

- *Challengers/disruptors* to zinc balance in the body (factors or substances that can impede the absorption or levels of nutrients in the body): zinc levels during conception and pregnancy, giving birth to twins or siblings in close proximity,* not being breastfed, iron supplementation, antibiotics, trauma, restrictive eating (avoiding meat, dairy and shellfish in particular), social isolation, phytate levels in plant foods, alcohol, drugs, smoking, copper coil and medications.

- *Consider also:* personal and family medical history, vegetarian and vegan diets, colic, fertility problems, postnatal depression in the birth mother, alcoholism, autoimmune, skin, thyroid, bowel, breast, lung and respiratory diseases, ASD (autism spectrum disorder), diabetes, mental health, eating disorders, Alzheimer's and dementia.

---

* Note: Twins and multiple-birth babies share the mother's zinc levels so are at greater risk of deficiency. The same risk is apparent when a new baby is conceived within 22 months of their older sibling. Breastfeeding can further deplete a mother's zinc reserves, while the zinc content of breast milk is also influenced by the mother's diet. If a breastfeeding mother has a zinc deficiency herself, it will impact the zinc content in her breast milk. Additionally, multiple-birth infants are less likely to be breastfed, and if they are, the duration is often limited. This is a prime example of how a baby's nutrient bank balance can be low or in debit from birth.

- *Signs and symptoms relating to iron imbalance:* feeling weak or tired, headaches, problems concentrating or thinking, irritability, loss of appetite, numbness and tingling of hands and feet, blue tinge to the whites of the eyes, brittle nails, desire to eat ice or frozen peas, light-headedness when standing up, pale skin colour, shortness of breath, sore or inflamed tongue and mouth ulcers.
- *Challengers/disruptors:* poor iron absorption, a deficiency or excess in the minerals zinc and/or copper, calcium supplementation, restricted eating, coeliac disease, Crohn's disease, ulcerative colitis, gastritis, gastrointestinal bleeding, high phytate levels in plant foods, heavy blood loss and some medications (e.g. protein pump inhibitors).
- *Consider also:* personal and family medical history, vegetarian and vegan diets, chronic kidney disease and heart disease, and considering any associated with zinc deficiency as above.
- *Signs and symptoms relating to copper imbalance:* pale skin, fatigue, frequent infections, numbness, tingling, difficulty with coordination, changes in hair and skin pigmentation, bone abnormalities.
- *Challengers/disruptors:* excess iron or zinc levels, high-dose vitamin C supplements, excessive dietary fibre, restricted eating, coeliac disease, inflammatory bowel disease, high phytate levels and oxalates in plant foods, and some medications (e.g. antacids containing aluminium).
- *Consider also:* personal and family medical history, anaemia, vegetarianism, veganism, osteoporosis, inflammatory bowel disease, neurological disorders, Menkes disease and Wilson disease.

B-vitamin deficiency
Key to higher energy and reducing anxiety

Many of my clients present with low energy levels and increased anxiety due to disturbances in the 'trinity of gut health'. Both zinc and iron enhance the synthesis of the B vitamins which power metabolism and support the nervous system. Although B_{12} and folate deficiency are commonly monitored in blood tests, little consideration is given to the rest of the B vitamins which work best as the 'B complex' team. As water-soluble vitamins that cannot be stored, the B vitamins need daily replenishment. This is particularly crucial for those with active lifestyles, insufficient intake of whole grains and leafy greens, or those who find themselves burning the candle at both ends. Recent scientific findings have shown that frequently undiagnosed MTHFR and FUT2 gene variants contributing to poor methylation can also disrupt B_{12} and folate utilization. it is also important to supplement with bioavailable forms of B_{12} such as methylcobalamin and andenosylcobalamin for B_{12} and methylfolate for folate, rather than non-bioavailable forms like cynanocobalamin and folic acid. In some cases, B_{12} injections may be necessary for optimal absorption.

- *Signs and symptoms of B-complex deficiency:* low energy levels, skin rashes, crack in the corner of the mouth, twitchy eyes, difficulty relaxing, pins and needles, restless legs, dark circles under the eyes, PMS, low self-esteem, procrastination, anxiety, low motivation, tired on waking, bloating, mood swings, brain fog, painful joints, glandular fever, panic attacks and chronic fatigue.
- *Challengers/disruptors:* zinc and copper levels, poor methylation (B_{12} and folate), the contraceptive pill, certain medications, drugs, carbonated drinks, alcohol, stress, exercise, ultra-processed baked goods, insufficient whole grains and leafy greens, and vegan and vegetarian diet. No laughing matter, increased recreational use of nitrous oxide (or laughing gas) is known to result in B_{12} deficiency: it can inactivate B_{12} by converting it to a form that the body cannot use and can cause serious neurological symptoms, anaemia and other health issues.
- *Consider also:* family medical history of anxiety, migraines, chronic fatigue, ME or myalgic encephalomyelitis, rheumatoid arthritis, high cholesterol, fibroids, cysts, liver disease, gallstones, gallbladder removal and vision problems.

Magnesium
Key to gut and mental health, enhanced energy, better sleep, reduced anxiety and stress

Magnesium (also called 'nature's stress-buster') helps regulate hundreds of body systems, including blood pressure, blood sugar, and muscle and nerve function. It also supports neuroplasticity in the brain and helps regulate dopamine, serotonin, GABA (gamma-aminobutyric acid) and melatonin, which are all key to restful sleep and healthy psychological function.

Modern farming practices and soil depletion have made it increasingly difficult to get sufficient levels of magnesium through our natural food sources, so deficiency is prevalent today. Furthermore, the higher the sugar and alcohol content in the diet, the more stressed the body becomes, while the more we exercise and the less we sleep, the greater the drain on the body's magnesium reserves, yet again increasing the likelihood of deficiency.

Magnesium also works closely with B complex to promote normal functioning of the nervous system.

Working in conjunction with calcium and vitamin D, magnesium helps maintain healthy bones and teeth. These three essential nutrients, supported by zinc, copper and phosphorus, form what I term the 'trinity of bone health' – a prerequisite for ensuring optimal bone density and guarding against osteoporosis in later life. While calcium excites and tightens muscles and blood vessels, magnesium relaxes and expands them.

- *Signs and symptoms of deficiency:* muscle aches and cramps, headaches, IBS (or irritable bowel syndrome), constipation, diarrhoea, PMS/PMT, craving salt and sugar, teeth grinding, irritability, acid reflux, thrush, cystitis, visuospatial problems, insomnia, lethargy, SAD (or seasonal affective disorder), impulsivity, poor attention and hyperactivity.
- *Challengers/disruptors:* soil depletion, high sugar and salt diet, calcium supplementation, stress, medications, drugs, soda drinks, alcohol, exercise, an ultra-processed diet, and insufficient whole grains, nuts, seeds and leafy greens.
- *Consider also:* personal and family medical history of diabetes, obesity, ADHD (or attention deficit hyperactivity disorder), cardio-vascular health, dental and bone health, strokes, vascular dementia, kidney stones, chronic kidney disease, osteoarthritis, hearing problems, Raynaud's disease, high blood pressure, Parkinson's disease, multiple sclerosis.

Vitamin D
Key to optimal gut, immune and mental health

Vitamin D deficiency is very common in young people.* This essential fat-soluble vitamin facilitates calcium absorption in the body, contributing to the building and maintenance of healthy bones and muscles. Additionally, it is integral to the efficient functioning of the immune system and promotes a balance of beneficial gut bacteria, to maintain gut lining integrity and reduce gut inflammation. Vitamin D requires magnesium for activation and is crucial in regulating calcium levels. While natural sunlight is the primary source of vitamin D for the average person, oily fish and eggs are the main natural dietary sources. It is also found in some mushrooms and certain fortified foods, especially milk and cereals (check the label).

- *Challengers/disruptors:* lack of exposure to natural sunlight, high SPF sun lotion, high omega-6 intake, alcohol, smoking, stress, medications, working or living in a basement and darker skin types.
- *Consider also:* family genetics and heritage, low immunity, autoimmune diseases, inflammatory disorders, depression, diabetes, metabolic disorders.

Essential fatty acids: omega-3, -6 (and -9)
Key to cognitive, physical and mental health

Fat plays important roles at the cellular level in the body as it is an essential part of cell membranes, with different types of fat altering how the cell responds to metabolic processes, including inflammation, controlling gene expression in the cell and the production of protein.

The body requires two types of essential fatty acids, omega-3 (alpha-linolenic acid) and omega-6 (linoleic acid) for healthy functioning. These polyunsaturated fats perform essential roles in the production of hormones including the eicosanoids, which help regulate the immune system and nervous system, and the function of other hormones. The

---

* As a result of the vitamin D deficiency widely highlighted as a risk factor during Covid, I have found that some of my older clients in particular have been self-prescribing excessive levels of vitamin D, which can lead to hypercalcemia and a disruption of the calcium/magnesium balance. As the body stores vitamin D (unlike vitamins B and C), excess levels can occur.

body is not able to make essential fatty acids so we must get them through the foods we eat.

It is scientifically accepted that excess intake of omega-6, in relation to omega-3 fatty acids, can contribute to inflammation and chronic disease. While research indicates that the diets of our human ancestors had equal amounts of omega-6 and omega-3 fatty acids (1:1), contemporary Western diets register higher levels of omega-6 fatty acids, often at a ratio of approximately 17:1.[3]

For this reason, I generally refrain from recommending pre-blended oils marketing themselves as 'the perfect balance of omegas 3, 6 and 9', as these would only be suitable for those individuals not eating any fat in their diet.

Omega-6

Omega-6 fatty acids are most commonly found in olive oil, walnuts, safflower oil, hemp seeds, sunflower seeds, avocado oil, almonds, eggs and cashew nuts. While omega-6 fats provide energy, I recommend eating omega-6-rich foods in moderation and pairing them with sufficient omega-3 fatty acids from sources like fatty fish, nuts and seeds. When a healthier balance is achieved between omega-3 and omega-6, then omega-9s will naturally fall into place.

Omega-9

Omega-9 fatty acids, commonly found in olive oil, canola oil, avocado oil and hazelnuts, are not strictly essential oils like omega-3 and -6, as the body can produce them. However, they deserve attention as they have many health-promoting properties, especially extra virgin olive oil. These monounsaturated fats play a crucial role in promoting heart health by lowering LDL (or 'bad') cholesterol levels and increasing HDL (or 'good') cholesterol. Additionally, their anti-inflammatory properties contribute to overall cardiovascular health. Omega-9s may be beneficial for blood sugar management too as they can help improve insulin sensitivity and assist weight management by promoting a sense of fullness after eating.

Omega-3

Omega-3 fatty acids are integral to various aspects of health, including lipid metabolism, blood sugar regulation, cognitive function, mental wellbeing, and the overall health of our eyes, gut, liver, heart, joints and skin. Despite their vital role in cell functioning, growth and development, levels tend to be worryingly low in the diets of many children, adolescents and adults.

Omega-3 fatty acids come in three primary forms: DHA (docosahexaenoic acid), EPA (eicosapentaenoic acid) and ALA (alpha-linolenic acid). While oily fish and seafood are rich sources of DHA and EPA, plant-based sources such as flaxseeds, chia seeds and walnuts are rich in ALA. Although the human body can convert ALA into EPA and DHA, this conversion rate is low and so to ensure optimum omega-3 levels, it is advisable to incorporate a variety of dietary sources, most especially those rich in DHA and EPA.

Inflammation is the body's natural response to infection or injury and involves the activation of the immune system. Chronic inflammation, often at low levels, is associated with depression and many physical health conditions, including eczema, cardiovascular disease, diabetes and autoimmune diseases.

Omega-3 fatty acids possess important anti-inflammatory properties too. While much research supports the role of omega-3 in helping to improve cardiovascular health, reduce inflammation and support cognitive function, one particular study on communities within prisons found that prisoners given omega-3 supplements are less irritable, angry and hostile, also beneficial for attention-deficit behaviour.[4]

Traditionally, depression, often co-morbid with anxiety, aggression, violence and self-harm, has been viewed as a disorder involving neurotransmitter imbalances, particularly involving serotonin, norepinephrine and dopamine. Commonly prescribed antidepressant medications, such as selective serotonin reuptake inhibitors (SSRIs), target these neurotransmitter systems and can disrupt gut health in the process. However, there has been a positive shift recently, with researchers increasingly exploring the role of inflammation in the development and progression of depression; that inflammation of the body can induce changes in how the brain functions, subsequently influencing cognition, mood and behaviour – factors we associate with depression.[5]

To ensure minimum threshold, I recommend my vegetarian and vegan clients in particular suplliments with a high-quality algae based Omega-3 supplement, which provides excellent levels of essential fatty acids DHA and EPA.

- *Signs and symptoms:* skin rash, scaly skin, dermatitis, hair loss, slow wound healing, decreased growth.
- *Challengers/disruptors (to omega-3):* a diet high in saturated and trans fats, too much omega-6, alcohol, smoking, stress, inflammatory bowel disease, coeliac disease, cystic fibrosis and certain medications.
- *Consider also:* personal and family history of inflammation, high cholesterol, depression, heart disease, liver disease, gallbladder problems, eyesight problems, diabetes, obesity and metabolic disorders.

Protein

I like to compare amino acids (the building blocks of protein) to the Lego brick as they are essential for the body's build and repair works. Protein is widely found in lean meats, poultry, fish, eggs, dairy products like milk, cheese, yoghurt and kefir, as well as in legumes and nuts. It is crucial for promoting muscle growth but also aiding in tissue repair and the synthesis of enzymes and hormones. Unfortunately, a significant number of young people consume insufficient protein for their daily requirements, which can lead to adverse effects such as slowed growth, muscle weakness, imbalances in blood sugar levels and increased cravings for sugary foods. Ensuring an adequate intake of protein is essential to support these foundational aspects of health and wellbeing.

Efficient protein synthesis can be challenged by various factors. Insufficient intake of essential amino acids and other nutrients, particularly with age, can hinder the body's ability to build proteins. Chronic illnesses affecting digestion and nutrient absorption, physical inactivity, hormonal imbalances, stress-induced cortisol elevation, inflammation, medications and inadequate sleep can all disrupt the intricate mechanisms of protein synthesis. Additionally, dehydration may compromise the efficiency of cellular functions, including the synthesis of vital proteins.

A holistic approach to health encompassing a balanced diet, regular movement, stress management and adequate sleep is crucial for optimizing protein synthesis and enhancing overall wellbeing.

- *Challengers/disruptors:* deficiency in zinc, copper, B_6, B_{12}, folate, sulphur and magnesium especially; high carbohydrate intake, vegetarian and vegan diets, restricted eating.

Rewilding the gut microbiome
Key to overall cognitive, physical and mental health

The gut microbiome refers to the diverse community of microorganisms, including bacteria, viruses, fungi and other microbes, that inhabit our digestive tract. The majority of the estimated 100 trillion microorganisms or microbiota reside in the colon, the large intestine at the lower part of the gastrointestinal tract. They are essential for numerous human metabolic activities, and their influence has been found to extend far beyond the digestive tract.

In a healthy body, disease-promoting pathogenic and symbiotic microbes (benefiting both the human body and microbiota) coexist happily. However, any disruption to this balance causes gut dysbiosis, resulting in a disruption of normal interactions that can leave the body more susceptible to disease.

Most of the pathogenic microorganisms are kept in check by the vast majority of symbiotic microbes inhabiting various parts of the body, including the skin and gastrointestinal tract. Our body's relationship with our microbes is symbiotic because it is mutually beneficial: our microbiota contribute to essential functions such as nutrient metabolism, immune system regulation and protection against harmful pathogens. It acts as a crucial ally in maintaining the overall health of the host organism (our body) by promoting a balanced and well-regulated internal environment. With this intricate balance, the body thrives, leveraging the positive contributions of symbiotic microorganisms while preventing the overgrowth or harmful effects of potential disease-causing pathogens.

The microbiome plays myriad roles in ensuring the smooth daily functioning of the human body, including:

- digesting our food
- producing metabolites, like short-chain fatty acids and vitamins, which strengthen the gut barrier and regulate and promote a healthy immune system
- protecting against other disease-causing bacteria by plugging the gaps in the intestinal barrier or 'crowding them out'
- breaking down potentially toxic food compounds
- helping to regulate hormone levels, including the amount of oestrogen circulating in the body
- producing neurotransmitters that affect how we feel, including dopamine, serotonin, norepinephrine and gamma-aminobutyric acid – all key players in triggering intense feelings of happiness, reward and a sense of calm
- synthesizing certain vitamins and amino acids, including B vitamins (B_{12}, thiamine and riboflavin) and vitamin K, which is needed for blood coagulation
- influencing the health of our skin, our respiratory system, our brain and our cognitive, emotional and mental health
- reducing inflammation in the body.

Aside from family genes, environment and medication use, diet plays an essential role in determining the types of bacteria that live in the colon, with certain nutrients, vitamins and minerals being required as co-factors.

Limosilactobacillus reuteri

In essence, *L. reuteri* is like the referee on the microbiome pitch, as it is a key modulator and 'gatekeeper' in the gut, helping to boost the proliferation of other good bacteria while also enabling the production of T-cells for the body's immune defence. This said, some scientific studies are showing a possible connection between various health conditions and very low levels or complete absence of *L. reuteri*.

I first became interested in *L. reuteri* when a notable research study found the microbe to be low and often absent in the microbiomes of ulcerative colitis (UC) patients.[6] This was hardly surprising given that many UC patients are routinely told to avoid dairy products and raw foods (such as sauerkraut and kimchi), which are among the few natural sources of *L. reuteri*. However, in my own health and that of many of my young clients with inflammatory bowel disease (IBD), rewilding *L. reuteri* in the microbiome has been transformative in helping to facilitate and maintain remission. Aside from physical improvements, many parents and carers can report a marked improvement in their child's social anxiety, with increased confidence and social engagement after rewilding the gut with *L. reuteri*.

In humans, *L. reuteri* is found in the stomach and upper gastrointestinal tract, the urinary tract, mouth and skin and in breast milk, however, it is increasingly facing extinction. This is notably evident in the microbiomes of those living in Western industrialized countries such as the UK, the USA and Canada – those same countries that have some of the highest populations of those with IBD. In the 1960s (when it was discovered), *L. reuteri* occurred naturally in the bodies of 30–40 per cent of the population. Today, it is found in just 10–20 per cent, with some reports showing it in as low as 4 per cent of the population.[7]

This decline can be attributed to the introduction of refrigeration and a decline in the consumption of fermented foods, antibiotics, excessive sanitation, exposure to chemicals and the prevalence of processed Western diets. However, *L. reuteri*'s vanishing is so remarkable that, in 2022, the University of Alberta launched clinical trials to rewild the bacteria in the microbiomes of Canadian citizens.[8,9]

Studies have also found that social isolation reduces our exposure to good bacteria. Research on animals and humans has found that *L. reuteri* can reduce social deficit by enhancing oxytocin production in the brain. In fact, it elevated blood oxytocin levels by over 300 per cent, boosting feelings of love and bonding in the same way that its presence in breast milk does.[8,9]

Challengers/disruptors:

- not breastfed or breastfed for a limited time and certain medical interventions at birth such as induced births and cesarean sections
- deficiency in intake of fermented foods (kefir, bio yoghurt, certain cheeses, kimchi, kombucha, miso and sauerkraut, etc.)
- increased intake of artificial sweeteners (widely used in diet foods, soda drinks and medications)
- increasingly homogeneous diet endangering plant-food species and diversity

- increased intake of processed foods that are high in animal fat and sugar
- lack of fibre and prebiotic foods in the diet (e.g. resistant starch and pectin)
- antibiotic usage
- medications
- overuse of household cleaners
- exposure to toxic chemicals
- more virtual and less social interaction and less time in nature.

Other beneficial bacteria

While *L. reuteri* is the referee on the microbiome pitch, it would be remiss not to mention other star players, including *Lactobacillus* and *Bifidobacterium* species and *Akkermansia muciniphila*. Collectively, these other types of good bacteria contribute to the balance and functionality of the gut microbiome. They strengthen our immune health and are beneficial for our overall health and wellbeing.

A lack of these essential bacteria has been found to be especially disadvantageous to health, and much of my work now involves rewilding these bacteria and educating young people on how to nurture them by eating more probiotic and prebiotic foods (see the list of recommended foods in the Appendix).

An analogy that resonates with my young clients involves posing a simple question: would you feed your cat a carrot or your dog a chocolate bar? By drawing this parallel, I encourage them to nurture their beneficial bacteria just as they care for their beloved pets, emphasizing the importance of providing specific foods that support the thriving health of these microscopic allies.

- *Lactobacillus:* commonly found in the digestive, oral, urinary and genital systems, *Lactobacillus* species ferment sugars into lactic acid which creates an environment that is unfavourable for many harmful bacteria. Some *Lactobacillus* species help synthesize vitamins and produce butyrate (see below).
- *Bifidobacterium:* these bacteria, also found in breast milk, are among the first to colonize an infant's gut and help establish a healthy microbiota. They inhabit the digestive system, especially the colon and mouth, where they work to break down complex carbohydrates,

promote the absorption of nutrients and prevent the growth of harmful bacteria.

Lactobacillus and *Bifidobacterium* are found in fermented milk kefir and yoghurt and plant products including sauerkraut, kimchi, miso, sourdough, and also in certain probiotic supplements.

Many gastrointestinal, immune or metabolic issues in my clients stem from insufficient butyrate (or butyric acid). Butyrate is a short-chain fatty acid and the main source of fuel for the cells (colonocytes) lining the colon. As well as having anti-inflammatory properties, these short-chain fatty acids ensure the gut remains oxygen-free, providing the optimum environment for our gut microbes to flourish.[10]

Certain species of *Lactobacillus* can produce butyrate. Acting as probiotics, butyrate-producing bacteria play important roles in balancing gut microbiota, maintaining the mucosal barrier, modulating the host immune response, preventing infections and regulating energy levels.

The easiest way to cultivate more butyrate-producing bacteria is to eat specific types of prebiotic and fibre-rich foods containing resistant starch and pectin. These also help nourish our other good bacteria, including the *Lactobacillus* and *Bifidobacterium* species. These include:

- asparagus
- bananas
- barley
- chicory root
- dandelion greens
- flaxseeds
- garlic
- leeks
- Jerusalem artichoke
- jicama root
- oats
- onions
- seaweed
- soybean
- yacon root
- wheat bran.

- *Akkermansia muciniphila:* this bacterium, the 'Pac-Man' of the gut, inhabits the mucous layer of the intestines and plays a key role in maintaining the integrity of the gut lining. It feeds on the mucin, the slimy mucous layer of the epithelial cells that cover the gut lining, a habitat shared by many other good bacteria. While this may sound counterintuitive, the more mucin *Akkermansia* eats, the more it encourages epithelial cells to make additional mucin. The more mucin you make, the stronger your intestinal wall and the healthier you are.

Akkermansia muciniphila has been linked to gut, metabolic and neuro-logical health and may have anti-inflammatory properties.[11] Research suggests that higher levels of *Akkermansia muciniphila* in the gut may be associated with a lower risk of obesity and metabolic disorders. Certain antioxidants known as polyphenols encourage the growth of *Akkermansia muciniphila* (see the list of recommended foods in the Appendix).

Notes

1. https://journals.plos.org/plosbiology/article?id=10.1371/journal.pbio.1002533
2. https://www.ncbi.nlm.nih.gov/pmc/articles/PMC7931793/
3. https://pubmed.ncbi.nlm.nih.gov/12442909/
4. https://www.researchgate.net/figure/Measures-of-Aggressive-and-Attention-Deficit-Behaviours-adjusted-T-scores-and-the_fig2_276911006 https://trialsjournal.biomedcentral.com/articles/10.1186/s13063-021-05252-2
5. https://www.ncbi.nlm.nih.gov/pmc/articles/PMC6158086/
6. https://www.ncbi.nlm.nih.gov/pmc/articles/PMC7270012/
7. https://clinicaltrials.gov/study/NCT03501082; https://www.sciencedaily.com/releases/2010/11/101102131302.htm#:~:text=In%20the%201960s%2C%20when%20the,found%20in%2010%2D20%20percent
8. https://www.ncbi.nlm.nih.gov/pmc/articles/PMC6645363/#:~:text=reuteri%20is%20able%20to%20reverse,idiopathic%20mouse%20models%20of%20ASD.
9. https://www.cell.com/cell/fulltext/S0092-8674(16)30730-9
10. https://www.clinicalnutritionjournal.com/article/S0261-5614(22)00384-3/fulltext
11. https://www.ncbi.nlm.nih.gov/pmc/articles/PMC9135416/

16

Molly's story

Rachel Ollerenshaw

Sometimes there's simply no reason why things happen. On Saturday, 2 September 2006 our lives changed forever after a normal fun family day out with our three children, Ben, five, Molly, three, and Maeve, two. After what seemed like an innocuous fall, Molly experienced severe discomfort which did not abate, and after some hours we brought her to our local A&E department.

Life completely changed for us then. We went from being a regular lively family living chaotic and (mostly) fun days, to learning after an ultrasound scan that Molly had a tumour in her left kidney. The paediatrician believed it to be a rare type of kidney cancer called a Wilms tumour, and Molly was immediately admitted to Birmingham Children's Hospital. Two weeks of tests and scans confirmed this diagnosis, and Molly immediately began a course of chemotherapy, followed by an operation to remove the affected kidney.

I recall feeling completely numb yet I continued to function, as I had to for the children. While we can empathize and listen to other people's stories of living through similar experiences, nothing ever prepares you for this same thing happening to you. So began a five-year journey with Molly undergoing numerous operations to remove tumours in one of her kidneys, on her bowel, in her liver and, finally, in her pelvis. She had every treatment possible: chemotherapy, radiotherapy, stem cell transplant and an endless list of other procedures. Through those years our lives revolved around hospital visits, blood tests and shielding ourselves from germs, avoiding crowds and not being able to enjoy the usual experiences of other young families.

In March 2011 we sat with our beautiful eight-year-old Molly and shared a conversation I never could have imagined anyone having with someone so young and innocent. But, Molly, like many children who face these challenges as I have since learned, had wisdom beyond her years. She always did, as she had a spirit, a deep knowing that was different from any other child I had met at that point. From the moment of diagnosis, Tim (Molly's dad) and I decided to be honest and fully transparent with Molly and her siblings, always explaining everything that was happening and encouraging them to ask questions in the hope that their understanding might make this journey a little less scary for them. I was glad we did, as that same year we were given the news that Molly's cancer had returned and that all treatment options were exhausted.

We spoke with Molly, offering her one of three available options: a clinical trial that was in its infancy with no certainty of outcome; chemotherapy that would give her more time; or doing nothing and living what was left of her young life. Molly chose the last and at the time I wondered whether a young child could truly understand the enormity of that choice. I know now that she did. A week after that conversation Molly and I were on the way to one of her schoolfriend's birthday parties when she turned to me in the car, saying, 'Mum, when I'm gone, can you make sure if Maeve has children that they get my *Flower Fairies* book.' Maeve was seven at the time.

Through her short life Molly taught us all so much. She knew she was dying and she took time to say her personal goodbyes to every one of us, family, friends and her school peers. I also realized that, by my being open and honest with her, she was less fearful. Yes, there was great sadness, but there was much calm too. Prior to Molly's terminal diagnosis I constantly worried about missing something, making sure the doctors checked everything, ensuring she had the best care. And she did.

Molly wanted to spend her last days at home where we were fantastically supported by our local community nursing team. Through my work now I often speak to other parents in the same situation and they worry about not being with their child at the end, asking me how to know when the end is coming. 'You just know' is always my reply. To this day I believe that the openness and trust Tim and I shared with our children and the acceptance of our hugely challenging situation helped us all enormously.

Naturally, Molly had moments of anger and frustration during her five-year journey, but for the most part she was calm, most especially towards the end of her life. She had a good death, if that is at all possible for a child so young. On 15 June 2011, Molly died at home in our arms and Ben and Maeve kissed their sister goodbye.

Molly had amazing spirit and determination and the impact she made in her very short years was astounding, as she touched the lives of friends and strangers alike and inspired so many good acts. All of this motivated us to create Molly Olly's Wishes in 2011. Through this charity Tim, Ben, Maeve and I keep Molly's spirit alive by supporting other children with life-threatening illnesses and their families during their darkest moments. Molly liked to shorten her own name from Molly Ollerenshaw to Molly Olly, hence Molly Ollys.

Losing a child goes against the usual order of life events, and in the UK we struggle to talk about the death of an adult, let alone a child. In the aftermath of Molly's passing, I experienced numerous reactions from others – the most hurtful was when people chose to ignore the fact, pretending it never happened, or would offer a quick thoughtless comment to get it out of the way for fear I might start wailing in public and cause a scene.

Many of those who looked us in the eyes saying Molly's name and talking about her and our grief had walked a similar path and were not afraid. It is always better to say something, even just to acknowledge Molly and our experience. We don't mind that you don't understand, as sadly the only way to really comprehend it is to have lived the experience for yourself.

No words can convey the depth of emotion we feel at losing a loved one, but being open and sharing our experiences through illness and in death and beyond can have a positive impact on how we live in our new world without these loved ones. Losing Molly has undoubtedly changed me. It has given me a greater thirst for what I would term 'real life'. Most of us will have something in our past that has impacted the way we live, and from opening up about our own experiences with Molly I have had the privilege of listening to other people's stories, some that would never have been shared previously, particularly stories told by the older generation who didn't have the opportunity to speak openly about grief and sadness as we do today. This made me realize, despite our loss, how lucky we are to have experienced Molly's love in our lives even for a short time.

A few years after Molly died, I was asked by a friend to speak publicly about the trauma we had experienced. However, my daughter Maeve was quick to correct us, highlighting that, while it was profoundly sad losing Molly, it wasn't 'trauma'. Molly was loved, supported and given the best care possible, so the panic, shock and anxiety around trauma were not present in the same way as they can be in many other situations. Hearing this from a young child highlighted how honest, open and age-appropriate communication can help reduce the deep stress associated with challenging situations. By ensuring we always discussed Molly's condition and treatment openly, even when those conversations were very difficult, it lessened the pain and distress.

I was acutely aware that my children's childhood was not as I had hoped and dreamed. I enjoyed a happy upbringing, full of love and fun. My own children had endured five years of their lives consumed by hospitals, missing out on everyday activities and losing some of the innocence of childhood, so after Molly died I made a conscious decision to embrace life as much as I could. This was never going to be easy as for a long time daily routines were an effort and grief was, and still can be, difficult to navigate. That said, losing Molly (and losing my mum when I was 29) taught me how precious every day really is. This doesn't mean I do anything wild or excessive. It just means I take huge pleasure in simple experiences, like sitting together around the dinner table, going to a movie, going for a walk and, above all, being content in the moment. We are a competitive family and always want to do the best we can, so to say that I am content and accepting of life may seem a contradiction, but I have learned that to constantly be at odds with what has happened would make me unhappy, with a knock-on effect on those around me.

Some things we cannot change, but accepting and finding a way to move forward helped me to enjoy life and not to sweat the small stuff. And I hope that this has also allowed Ben and Maeve to have a mum who is present.

Molly may have been with us for a very short time, but her legacy is significant for myriad reasons, mostly because her heart and mind were always big and open. Thank you, Molly.

Meet Molly Ollerenshaw. If Molly was still with us she would be 21 and bravely navigating this new world we call home.

All *Un:Stuck* advances and 50% of the book royalties will be donated to Molly Ollys, a charity created by Molly's mum, Rachel Ollerenshaw, to support children with life-threatening illnesses and their families across the UK.

17

Un:Stuck: flourishing

Kate O'Brien

'One of the most calming and powerful actions you can do to intervene in a stormy world is to stand up and show your soul. Soul on deck shines like gold in dark times. When a great ship is in harbor and moored, it is safe, there can be no doubt. But... that is not what great ships are built for...'

Clarissa Pinkola Estés, *Do Not Lose Heart,*
We Were Made for These Times[1]

So where do we go from here? First, we pause and we take a long deep breath...

No, we cannot just sit back or say 'it's just the way it is, I can't change it' because it isn't and you can. So much is on the line here for ourselves and for our children, and for their children. From this foundation of wisdom and science we come together and imagine the future we all, older and younger, want to live in.

In *The Lighthouse Effect: How ordinary people can have an extraordinary impact on the world*, Steve Pemberton uses his harrowing life story to highlight how ordinary people, wrestling with their own struggles and imperfections, can be the quiet heroes touching the lives of others. Pemberton writes:

> The human lighthouse is a beacon, something offering us hope and inspiration and guiding our journey. They are, at first glance, seemingly ordinary people going about their daily routines, but a closer look reveals that they are a lot more. Human lighthouses are steadfast and faithful, humble yet unwavering, always illuminating the pathway to hope and sanctuary. They summon us to a better understanding of ourselves and point us all toward a greater humanity.[2]

A theme that emerges strongly through the page of this book is community. Writing my own contribution and collaborating with my colleagues has taught me a lot for which I will be ever grateful. Most of all it has taught me what coming together really means, and it has showed me that the village we have been referring to over and over through these chapters is us, ourselves.

Good work is unfolding in every corner of the world and each of us has a role to play. No one said it would be easy or certain, but often in life the best outcomes take time and perseverance. This is our chance to show what it means not only to survive these turbulent times but to flourish and thrive, even in this polarized, divisive culture where many of our so-called leaders do not model who we can be as parents, as teachers, as employers and as architects of change. With this in mind, let's find our warrior spirits and chart this unmapped path together. We will stumble, and when we do, let's forgive one another's weaknesses and continue to lead with love, kindness and compassion.

In *The Dawn of a Mindful Universe*, Brazilian physicist Marcelo Gleiser writes:

> Each individual has a role to play. This role involves sacrifices that are entirely distinct from those of a bloody revolution. Instead of paying with our lives, we celebrate and preserve life and align our values and actions according to three principles: the LESS approach to sustainability, the MORE approach to engagement with the natural world, and the MINDFUL approach to consumerism.[3]

Ultimately, if we don't address these root causes of loneliness and deep unhappiness in the younger generation, who will, and what will the future hold? If you live life without a moral compass, it's hard to know where to go. Our children are watching our behaviour, so let us always remind them of a better way to be. And if you still believe that you are too small and insignificant to make a real difference, please remember that if we don't change, nothing changes. It's as simple as that. I urge you to become that beacon of hope and create your own 'lighthouse effect' as your strength becomes that bright shining beam for others. It doesn't have to be a big, ambitious thing. It may be small, personal and just as meaningful.

As Tiokasin Ghosthorse writes in Chapter 13: 'This is the hardest time to live, but it is also the greatest honour to be alive now, and to be allowed to see this time.' When times are hard or situations become frustrating, don't let us give up. It is past time for sitting on the side line waiting for someone else to do it.

In Ireland we have a particular word, *dán*, which weaves together the realms of poetry, talent and vocation. Our *dán* is our unique gift to the world, our destiny code that we were born to embody. These words moulded into chapters would not have been possible without the help and support of the many wise thinkers, teachers, academics, activists and visionaries who have shared their respective *dán* to give *Un:Stuck* its wings to soar. I am deeply grateful to you all. Your voices and insights are much needed.

Let's come together now and let's show the next generation a different way. If not us, then who? The time of the lone wolf is indeed over. This is our time. This could be a good time.

The Hopi Elders' Prophecy, 8 June 2000

Know your garden. It is time to speak your truth. Create your community. Be good to each other. And do not look outside yourself for your leader.

Then he clasped his hands together, smiled, and said, This could be a good time! There is a river flowing now very fast. It is so great and swift that there are those who will be afraid. They will try to hold on to the shore. They will feel they are being torn apart and will suffer greatly. Know the river has its destination. The elders say we must let go of the shore, push off into the middle of the river, keep our eyes open, and our heads above the water.

And I say, see who is in there with you and celebrate. At this time in history, we are to take nothing personally, least of all ourselves. For the moment that we do, our spiritual growth and journey come to a halt.

The time of the lone wolf is over. Gather yourselves! Banish the word 'struggle' from your attitude and your vocabulary. All that we do now must be done in a sacred manner and in celebration.

We are the ones we've been waiting for.

Note

1. https://moonmagazine.org/clarissa-pinkola-estes-do-not-lose-heart-we-were-made-for-these-times-2016-12-31/

2. Pemberton, Steve, *The Lighthouse Effect: How ordinary people can have an extraordinary impact on the world.* Zondervan, 2021.

3. Gleiser, Marcelo, *The Dawn of a Mindful Universe: A Manifesto for Humanity's Future*, HarperOne, 2023.

Appendix

Essential vitamin and mineral guide

Charlotte Fraser

The most common deficiencies noticed in puberty and young adults are in **bold**.

Vitamin/Mineral	Food sources	Important for
A (retinol) *Fat soluble* *Antioxidant*	Liver, oily fish (salmon, mackerel and trout), dairy (milk, cheese, butter), egg yolk, carrots, sweet potatoes, squash, pumpkin, leafy greens (spinach, kale, broccoli, collard greens), red bell peppers, cantaloupe melon, apricot and mango	Body tissue repair and maintenance Vision Healthy skin, hair and nails Fighting infection Immune system Cell differentiation Beta carotene, precursor to vitamin A, antioxidant benefits Reproductive health Anti-ageing Anti-inflammatory properties
B$_1$ (thiamine) *Water soluble*	Molasses, brewer's yeast, brown rice, fish, meat, nuts, liver, poultry, wheatgerm milk, potatoes, soya beans, peas	Metabolism (converts glucose into energy) Healthy nervous system Supports various cellular functions, including those related to blood cell production Cell respiration Growth, appetite and digestion Energy production in muscles Eye health Heart health Healthy digestion (hydrochloric acid) Normal liver function and detoxification Cognitive health and mental clarity

Vitamin/Mineral	Food sources	Important for
		Stress response Regulating moods
B$_2$ (riboflavin) *Water soluble*	Crude molasses, nuts, organic meats, wholegrains, milk, cheese, fish, yeast extract, eggs, bran, wheatgerm, avocado, potatoes	Antibody and red blood cell formation Production of adenosine triphosphate (ATP), the primary energy currency of cells Respiration Healthy skin, hair and nails
B$_3$ (niacin) *Water soluble*	Lean meat, white meat, oily fish and eggs	Energy metabolism and carbohydrates, fat and protein metabolism Healthy nervous system Healthy digestive system Brain function (cognition and memory) Heart health Healthy skin Joint mobility Cholesterol management Blood sugar management
B$_5$ (pantothenic acid) *Water soluble*	Brewer's yeast, legumes, salmon, trout, liver, wheatgerm, whole grains, eggs, chicken, turkey, nuts, seeds, oats, dairy (milk, cheese, yoghurt)	Nervous system support Reducing stress and anxiety Anti-inflammatory Aids antibody formation Carbohydrate, fat and protein conversion (energy) Growth and development Vitamin utilization (especially vitamin B$_2$) Detoxification of drugs Healthy skin

Vitamin/Mineral	Food sources	Important for
B₆ (pyridoxine acid) *Water soluble*	Crude molasses, brewer's yeast, leafy green vegetables, liver, wheatgerm, whole grains, fish, milk, eggs, sweet potatoes	Immune support (antibody formation) Metabolism of amino acids Regulation of hormones Mood regulation and sleep Overall nervous system function and synthesis of neurotransmitters such as serotonin, dopamine and GABA Digestion (hydrochloric acid production) Fat and protein utilization (weight management) Contributing to the production of antibodies, supporting the immune system. Aiding in the conversion of stored glycogen into glucose for energy Skin health
B₁₂ (cobalamin) *Water soluble*	Dairy (milk, cheese, yoghurt), fish, liver, eggs, beef, pork, cabbage, bean sprouts, fortified cereals, whole grains, banana, alfalfa, almonds	Appetite DNA synthesis Red blood cell formation Health and function of the nervous system, including the formation of myelin sheaths around nerves Energy metabolism Brain health Homocysteine regulation important for cardiovascular health Proper cell division and maintenance of healthy tissues Folate metabolism Bone health
Biotin *Water soluble*	Legumes, whole grains, liver, egg yolk, nuts, milk, brown rice, yeast, fish, strawberries, sweetcorn, hazelnuts	Cell growth Fatty acid production Metabolism Vitamin B utilization

Vitamin/Mineral	Food sources	Important for
Folic acid *Water soluble*	Green leafy vegetables, dairy products (milk, cheese, yoghurt), liver, oysters, salmon, fortified cereals, whole grains, egg yolk, lentils, avocado, courgettes, Brussel sprouts, spinach	Appetite DNA synthesis and repair Cell growth Neural tube development Red blood cell formation Hydrochloric acid production Protein metabolism Genetic transmission Infection resistance in new-born babies Homocysteine metabolism May be beneficial for mental health as involved in the synthesis of neurotransmitters, such as serotonin, important for mood regulation
C (ascorbic acid) *Water soluble* *Antioxidant*	Citrus fruits, kiwi fruit, honeydew melon, potatoes, Red, green and yellow bell peppers, broccoli, papayas, strawberries, rosehips, blackcurrants, tomatoes	Bone and tooth formation Collagen production Iodine conservation Healing (burns and wounds) Red blood cell formation Resistance to shock and infection Enhances the absorption of non-haem iron Aids B_{12} absorption Vitamin protection (oxidation)
Calcium	Milk, cheese, yoghurt, green vegetables, kefir, milk, nuts, seeds, soya beans, sardines, salmon, quinoa	Strong bones and teeth Regulating heartbeat Sleep Muscle contraction and relaxation Neurotransmission Cell signalling Blood clotting Enzyme activation Cell division and regulation of the cell cycle Hormone secretion, including insulin Vascular tone, influencing blood vessel constriction and dilation Acid-base balance maintenance Co-factor for ATP production (energy currency of the cell) Absorption and metabolism of various minerals and vitamins

Vitamin/Mineral	Food sources	Important for
Chromium	Meat, shellfish, brewer's yeast	Blood sugar balance and glucose metabolism Enhances insulin sensitivity Supporting carbohydrate and lipid metabolism Potentially contributes to weight management Aids in energy production Facilitates protein synthesis Regulates blood glucose levels
Copper *Antioxidant*	Oysters and other shellfish, whole grains, beans, nuts, potatoes, organ meats (kidneys, liver). Also dark leafy greens, cocoa, black pepper, shiitake mushrooms, yeast	Red blood cell production Maintains healthy nerve cells Production of neurotransmitters Maintains healthy immune system Collagen formation Aids iron absorption Energy production (cellular respiration)
D *Fat soluble* *Antioxidant*	Liver, bone meal, sunlight, milk, salmon, tuna fish, mushrooms, fish oil and algae supplements	Aids calcium and phosphorus absorption (bone formation) Immune system Heart action Healthy nervous system Cell differentiation Health of epithelial tissue
E (tocopherol) *Fat soluble* *Antioxidant*	Dark green vegetables, eggs, liver organ meats, wheatgerm, vegetable oils, soya beans, whole wheat, lettuce	Ageing retardation, protects cells from damage caused by free radicals Anti-clotting factor Blood cholesterol reduction Enhancing blood flow to heart Strengthening blood capillary wall Fertility and male potency Protecting lungs (anti-pollution) Healthy muscles and nerves

Vitamin/Mineral	Food sources	Important for
Essential fatty acids	Algae, chia, flax, hemp and linseeds, oily fish, pumpkin seeds, vegetable oils, walnuts	Healthy brain and cell formation Immune system Healthy nervous system Omega-3 specific: • normal brain function • development of foetus and breastfed infants Maintains normal function of the heart and blood pressure Blood concentrations of triglycerides Blood cholesterol levels Vision Cell membrane integrity Skin health Joint health Normal liver function May be beneficial for boosting mental health and preventing depression
Iodine	Whole cow's milk and yoghurt, seafood, kelp, iodized salt, fortified plant-based milks	Energy production Metabolism Physical and mental health Formation of thyroxine for thyroid function
Iron	Crude molasses, eggs, fish, lean red meat (especially beef), poultry, wheatgerm, soya flour, curry powder, spinach, raisins, peas, lentils, quinoa, legumes, apricots	Stress management Immune function and disease resistance Essential for oxygen transport and energy production Cellular growth DNA synthesis Proper brain function Detoxification processes Contributing to antioxidant enzyme function
K (menadione) *Fat soluble*	Green leafy vegetables, kelp, safflower oil, molasses, yoghurt, oatmeal, liver, fish, soya beans, beef, tomatoes	Blood clotting (coagulation) Normal liver function Bone density Healthy brain and heart Anti-inflammatory

Vitamin/Mineral	Food sources	Important for
Magnesium	Apples, apricots, fish (mackerel, salmon and halibut), green leafy vegetables (spinach, Swiss chard, kale), collard greens, lima beans, nuts (esp. almonds), peaches, seeds, soya beans, bone meal, kelp, tofu, honey, garlic, whole grains such as brown rice, oats, quinoa and whole wheat	Involved in over 200 essential metabolic processes Stress reduction Co-factor for ATP production (the energy currency of the cell) Energy production Synthesis of protein and nucleic acids Formation of urea Vascular tone Muscle impulse transmissions Electrical stability of cells, neurotransmission and activity Acid/alkaline balance Regulation of insulin levels Blood sugar metabolism Conversion of tryptophan (an amino acid) into serotonin Healthy bones and teeth Proper functioning of muscles and normal nerve function Absorption and metabolism of other minerals and vitamins, including balancing calcium Anti-inflammatory properties; may help modulate inflammation in the nervous system May be beneficial for mental health and preventing depression
Manganese *Antioxidant*	Bananas, bran, celery, egg yolk, green leafy vegetables, legumes, liver, nuts, pineapples, whole grains	Enzyme activation Reproduction and growth Regulating blood sugar Cholesterol metabolism Sex hormone production Bone formation and health Tissue respiration Wound healing (collagen) Thyroid function Healthy joints (cartilage) Vitamin B_3 metabolism Vitamin E utilization Cofactor for certain antioxidant enzymes Neurological function Antioxidant defence

Vitamin/Mineral	Food sources	Important for
Molybdenum	Canned beans, liver, buckwheat, barley, oats, legumes, soya beans	Enzyme action Metabolism of purine and sulphur Production of uric acid Detoxification Antioxidant defence
Phosphorus	Eggs, fish, grains, meat, poultry, cheese, calves' liver, milk, yoghurt	Bone and tooth formation DNA and RNA synthesis Cell growth and repair Energy production Heart muscle contraction Healthy kidney function Metabolism (calcium, sugar) Nerve function and muscle contraction Vitamin utilization (B vitamins especially)
Potassium	Dates, figs, peaches, peanuts, raisins, seafood, apricots (dried), bananas, muesli, potato, avocado	Stabilizing heart rhythm Rapid cell growth and division for cellular health and tissue repair Regulating nerve impulses, contributing to the proper functioning and calmness of the nervous system Works with salt to regulate water balance in body Supports healthy muscle function, including the smooth muscles of digestive tract
Selenium *Antioxidant*	Brazil nuts, liver, beef, chicken, tuna, halibut, sardines, salmon, sunflower seeds, eggs, oats, wheat, tomatoes, mushrooms, onions, spinach and other leafy greens	Reducing oxidative stress Thyroid function Healthy elasticity of tissue Dandruff prevention Supports heart and liver function
Sulphur	Fish, eggs, cabbage, onions, garlic	Healthy hair, skin and nails Healthy cells Brain function (neurotransmitter synthesis)

Vitamin/Mineral	Food sources	Important for
Zinc *Antioxidant*	Shellfish, brewer's yeast, red meat, chicken, lentils, liver, nuts, pumpkin and squash seeds, shellfish, soya beans, spinach, sunflower seeds, whole grains	A constituent of more than 2,000 enzymes involved in digestion and metabolism Essential for gene expression and the synthesis of DNA Involved in the normal absorption and action of other vitamins, especially B vitamins and iron Acid-base metabolism Macronutrient metabolism Carbohydrate metabolism Normal cognitive function Fertility and reproduction Histamine regulation Hormone regulation Metabolism of fatty acids and vitamin A Iron absorption Protein synthesis Maintains healthy bones, hair, skin and nails Maintains healthy testosterone levels in the blood Maintains healthy vision Immune system regulation Inhibition of inflammatory mediators; may be beneficial for mental health and preventing depression Glutathione synthesis Protection of cells from oxidative stress Healthy cell division; growth and development Healthy thyroid function Improves stability of oxytocin hormone Synthesis, storage and secretion of insulin

Further reading

Bates, Tony. *Breaking the Heart Open: The shaping of a psychologist*. Gill Books, 2023

Brach, Tara. *Radical Acceptance: Awakening the love that heals fear and shame.* Rider, 2003

Britton, Easkey. *Saltwater in the Blood: Surfing, natural cycles, and the sea's power to heal.* Watkins Publishing, 2021

Britton, Easkey. *Ebb and Flow: Connect with the patterns and power of water.* Watkins Publishing, 2023

Brown, Brené. *Daring Greatly: How the courage to be vulnerable transforms the way we live, love, parent, and lead.* Penguin Life, 2015

Brown, Brené. *The Gifts of Imperfection.* Hazelden Publishing, 2022

Carson, Rachel. *Silent Spring.* Penguin, 2000

Chödrön, Pema. *The Places that Scare You: A guide to fearlessness.* Harper NonFiction, 2004

Chödrön, Pema. *Start Where You Are: How to accept yourself and others.* Element Books, 2005

Chödrön, Pema. *When Things Fall Apart: Heart advice for difficult times.* Harper NonFiction, 2005

Cole, Lily. *Who Cares Wins: How to protect the planet you love: a thousand ways to solve the climate crisis: from tech-utopia to indigenous wisdom.* Penguin Life, 2021

Damour, Lisa. *The Emotional Lives of Teenagers.* Allen & Unwin, 2023

Dusick, Ryan. *Harder to Breathe: A memoir of making Maroon 5, losing it all, and finding recovery.* Penguin Random House, 2022

Ehrenfeld, John R. *Sustainability by Design: A subversive strategy for transforming our consumer culture.* Yale University Press, 2008

Frankl, Viktor E. *Man's Search for Meaning: The classic tribute to hope from the Holocaust.* Rider, 2004

Gennari, Anne Therese. *The Climate Optimist Handbook: How to shift the narrative on climate change and find the courage to choose change.* Aviva Publishing, 2022

Gilio-Whitaker, Dino. *As Long as Grass Grows: The indigenous fight for environmental justice, from colonization to Standing Rock.* Beacon Press, 2019

Gleason, David. *At What Cost?: Defending adolescent development in fiercely competitive schools.* Developmental Empathy LLC, 2017

Gleiser, Marcelo. *The Dawn of a Mindful Universe: A manifesto for humanity's future.* HarperOne, 2023

Grant, Adam. *Hidden Potential: The science of achieving greater things.* WH Allen, 2023

Halifax, Joan. *Standing at the Edge: Finding freedom where fear and courage meet.* Flatiron Books, 2019

Hari, Johann. *Stolen Focus: Why you can't pay attention.* Bloomsbury, 2023
Hawken, Paul. *Regeneration: Ending the climate crisis in one generation.* Penguin, 2021
HH Dalai Lama and Cutler, Howard C. *The Art of Happiness: A handbook for living.* Hodder, 1999
Hübl, Thomas and Avritt, Julie Jordan. *Healing Collective Trauma: A process for integrating our intergenerational and cultural wounds.* Sounds True, 2023
Hutchins, Giles and Storm, Laura. *Regenerative Leadership: The DNA of life-affirming 21st century organizations.* Wordzworth Publishing, 2019
Johnson, Anaya Elizabeth and Wilkinson, Katharine K. *All We Can Save: Truth, courage and solutions for the climate crisis.* One World, 2021
Kabat-Zinn, Jon. *Full Catastrophe Living: How to cope with stress, pain and illness using mindfulness meditation.* Piatkus, 2013
Kimmerer, Robin Wall. Braiding *Sweetgrass: Indigenous wisdom, scientific knowledge and the teachings of plants.* Penguin, 2020
Kumar, Satish. *Elegant Simplicity: The art of living well.* New Society Publishers, 2019
Kumar, Satish. *Radical Love: From separation to connection with the earth, each other, and ourselves.* Parallax Press, 2023
Lerner, Harriet. *The Dance of Connection: How to talk to someone when you're mad, hurt, scared, frustrated, insulted, betrayed, or desperate.* William Morrow & Company, 2002
Lockley, John. *Leopard Warrior: A journey into the African teachings of ancestry, instinct, and dreams.* Sounds True, 2017
Macartney, Mac. *Finding Earth, Finding Soul: The invisible path to authentic leadership.* Green Books, 2007
Macartney, Mac. *The Children's Fire: Heart song of a people.* Practical Inspiration Publishing, 2018
Maté, Gabor and Neufeld, Gordon. *Hold on to Your Kids: Why parents need to matter more than peers.* Vermilion, 2019
Menaken, Resmaa. *My Grandmother's Hands: Racialized trauma and the pathway to mending our hearts and bodies.* Penguin, 2021
Miller, Lisa. *The Awakened Brain: The psychology of spirituality and our search for meaning.* Penguin, 2021
Moore, Phillip. *The Future of Children: Providing a love-based education for every child.* Emergence Education, 2017
Ngomane, Nompumelelo Mungi. *Everyday Ubuntu: Living better together the African way.* Bantam Press, 2019
Nichols, Dr Wallace J. *Blue Mind: The surprising science that shows how being near, in, on, or under water can make you happier, healthier, more connected, and better at what you do.* Back Bay Books, 2015
Paull, Laline. *Pod.* Corsair, 2023
Pemberton, Steve. *The Lighthouse Effect: How ordinary people can have an extraordinary impact on the world.* Zondervan, 2021

Perry, Bruce D. and Winfrey, Oprah. *What Happened To You?: Conversations on trauma, resilience, and healing.* Flatiron Books 2021

Perry, Philippa. *The Book You Wish Your Parents Had Read (and Your Children Will Be Glad that You Did).* Penguin Life, 2020

Phaidon Editors, with an introduction by Melster, Anne-Marie. *Ocean: Exploring the marine world.* Phaidon Press, 2022

Pueblo, Yung. *Lighter: Let go of the past, connect with the present, and expand the future.* Penguin, 2022

Robinson, Ken. *Out of Our Minds: Learning to be creative.* Capstone, 2011

Robinson, Ken. *Finding Your Element: How to discover your passions and talents and transform your life.* Penguin, 2014

Siegel, Daniel J. *IntraConnected: MWe (Me + We) as the integration of self, identity, and belonging.* W W Norton & Co, 2022

Singer, Michael A. *Untethered Soul: The journey beyond yourself.* New Harbinger Publications, 2007

Singer, Michael A. *The Surrender Experiment: My journey into life's perfection.* Yellow Kite, 2016

Slijepcevic, Predrag B. *Biocivilisations: A new look at the science of life.* Chelsea Green Publishing Co, 2023

Spargo-Mabbs, Fiona. *I Wish I'd Known: Young people, drugs and decisions – a guide for parents and carers.* Sheldon Press, 2021

Spargo-Mabbs, Fiona. *Talking the Tough Stuff with Teens: Making conversations work when it matters most.* Sheldon Press, 2022

Sri Narayani Peedam. *Connect with The Divine Vol 1.* Sri Narayani Peedam, 2014

Thunberg, Greta. *The Climate Book.* Allen Laine, 2022

Tolle, Eckhart. *The Power of Now: A guide to spiritual enlightenment.* Yellow Kite, 2001

Turkle, Sherry. *Alone Together: Why we expect more from technology and less from each other,* 3rd edn. Basic Books, 2011

Wright, Bonnie. *Go Gently: Actionable steps to nurture yourself and the planet.* Greenfinch, 2022

Wolynn, Mark. *It Didn't Start with You: How inherited family trauma shapes who we are and how to end the cycle.* Vermilion, 2022

Contributors

Kate O'Brien

Born in Galway, Ireland, Kate has been working and living in the wellbeing space for over 30 years, combining her scientific, nutrition and yoga teaching qualifications to help others along their unique journey to health, wellbeing and joy. She is an honours science graduate and a qualified dietitian with a post-graduate diploma in cosmetic science and a 200-hour Yoga Alliance teaching qualification. Kate continues to write in global publications and and is frequently interviewed on global media. She is the author of nine lifestyle books, including *Your Middle Years* and *GLOW: Your complete four-week plan to healthy radiant skin*.

Charlotte Fraser

Charlotte Fraser is a naturopathic nutritionist with over 20 years' experience working in the nutrition, health and wellness sector in the UK. She specializes in adolescent and young adult nutrition and is founder of The Whole Student, a programme providing holistic health and wellbeing support to secondary school students. She holds a Diploma in Naturopathic Nutrition and Food Intolerance Testing, and a TQUK Level 2 Certificate in 'Understanding Behaviour that Challenges'. Her interest in the gut–brain axis led her to delve into psychodynamic and transpersonal psychotherapy, ancient healing practices and mindfulness.

    www.naturopathic-nutrition.com

Easkey Britton

Dr Easkey Britton is a renowned Irish surfer, author, artist and marine social scientist from Rossnowlagh, Co. Donegal, Ireland, with a deep love and passion for tapping into the healing powers of the sea. She specializes in the interdependencies between the ocean and humans, contributing her expertise in 'blue health' on national and international research projects. She is the author of several books on our human relationship with water, including *50 Things to Do by the Sea*, her memoir *Saltwater in the Blood* (2021) and most recently *Ebb and Flow: Connect with the patterns and power of water* (2023), a feminist reimagining of the meaning of power through the lens of water.

https://easkeybritton.com/

Ed Olver

Growing up overseas and educated in the UK, Ed Olver enjoyed a broad and illuminating professional life in finance and the military before becoming an entrepreneur in commercial foreign policy, technology and government advisory. Ed is now committed to aligning his spiritual and professional experience through the sacredlands.life platform for Soil, Soul and Service, Visions For The Future series at Broughton Sanctuary.

https://sacredlands.life/

Fiona Spargo-Mabbs OBE

Fiona Spargo-Mabbs is director and founder of the Daniel Spargo-Mabbs Foundation drug education charity. With over 20 years' experience working in education as a teacher, manager and national lead working with vulnerable families, Fiona co-founded the DSM Foundation in 2014 in response to the death of her 16-year-old son Daniel having taken ecstasy. She works directly with young people, parents and professionals and in 2023 was awarded an OBE for services to young people. Fiona is author of *I Wish I'd Known: Young people, drugs and decisions – a guide for parents and carers* and *Talking the Tough Stuff with Teens: Making conversations work when it matters most* (both Sheldon Press).

www.dsmfoundation.org.uk

Galahad Clark

Galahad is a seventh-generation cobbler. As a teenager, he spent summer holidays on shoe production lines in Europe and Asia learning the family trade. After finishing school, he went to America on a Morehead scholarship to study Chinese and Anthropology where he also founded the charity Students for Students. In 2003, Galahad started his first shoe project, 'Wu Shoes', and later launched United Nude and Worn Again (a closed-loop green technology business) and Vivobarefoot, where he now focuses his energies. Galahad participates on various boards focused on helping humans reconnect back to nature. He is married to Bayarma and has two daughters.

https://www.vivobarefoot.com/eu/

Judy Blaine PhD

South African born and bred Dr Judy Blaine lived and worked in Hong Kong for 30 years where she raised her four children. She is a research fellow at both Hong Kong University and Rhodes University in South Africa. Much of her work and research focuses on psychosocial wellbeing, integrating empathy, equity, diversity, inclusion, nature connection, indigenous ways of knowing and social justice. Judy founded her own company, Odyssey, which offers a strength-based approach to help young individuals reach their full potential.

https://odyssey.net.za/about/

Karl Sebire PhD

Dr Karl Sebire is a leading expert in technology dependence, digital distraction and screentime. With over 20 years' experience in the creative and education industries, Karl researches how teaching and learning have evolved to adapt to an audience who consume media in entirely new ways. As the ability to focus becomes the emerging differentiator for individuals, Karl writes, speaks and consults on how one can harness the myriad powers of technology while attenuating the many challenges it presents.

https://www.karlsebire.com/

Mac Macartney

Mac Macartney is an author, peace advocate and international speaker. He is the founder of Embercombe in the UK, a centre that seeks to inspire and empower people to live in close relationship with nature and co-create a regenerative, flourishing future for all species. For over

20 years Mac was mentored by indigenous elders and continues to strive to merge the ancient emphasis on relationship, interdependence and reverence for life with the significant challenges and opportunities of the twenty-first century. He is a former member of Danone North America's Advisory Committee, has sat on sustainability advisory panels for large organizations and is the author of two books.

www.macmacartney.com

Mary Lyn Campbell

Born in Scotland and living in Zurich, Mary Lyn has over 30 years experience at the tertiary, secondary and primary levels of education. She was Head of School at the Inter-Community School Zurich for 10 years and is former Principal/Head of School at The British Schools in Montevideo, Uruguay. Prior to this, she was Associate Academic Dean of the School of Business at the Universidad de Montevideo, Uruguay. She holds a Bachelor's degree from Duke University, a Master's degree from Johns Hopkins University and is the S.T.A.R. (Special Teachers Are Recognized) award recipient from Cornell University, New York. She was a participant at the first "Future of Learning" workshop at Harvard Graduate School of Education and is an experienced CIS (Council of International Schools) and NEASC (New England Association of Schools and Colleges) Accreditation Team Leader. Mary Lyn is currently piloting a new project on Wellness and Happiness certification for International Schools. She has been interviewed on TV and her written work been quoted in global publications.

Mindahi Bastida

Born in Tultepec, Mexico, Mindahi is a member of the Otomi-Toltec Nation of Mexico. He is the chief staff holder of the Grand Council of the Eagle and the Condor. Mindahi holds a doctorate in rural development from the Universidad Autónoma Metropolitana and has written extensively on the relationship between the state and indigenous peoples, intercultural education, collective intellectual property rights and associated traditional knowledge.

Ryan Dusick, MA, AMFT

Ryan Dusick is an associate marriage and family therapist, the founding drummer of Maroon 5, a mental health coach, speaker and author of *Harder to Breathe: A memoir of making Maroon 5, losing it all, and finding recovery*. He holds a master's degree in clinical psychology from Pepperdine University and a bachelor's degree from UCLA.
https://www.ryandusick.com/

Tiokasin Ghosthorse

Tiokasin Ghosthorse is an indigenous activist and member of the Cheyenne River Lakota Nation of South Dakota. Tiokasin is the founder, host and executive producer of First Voices Radio (formerly First Voices Indigenous Radio) for the last 32 years in New York City and Seattle/Olympia, Washington. In 2016, he was nominated for the Nobel Peace Prize from the International Institute of Peace Studies and Global Philosophy and is the recipient of the Native Arts and Cultures Foundation National Fellowship in Music (2016), National Endowment for the Arts National Heritage Fellowship Nominee (2017), Indigenous Music Award Nominee for Best Instrumental Album (2019) and National Native American Hall of Fame Nominee (2018, 2019). He was nominated for the 2020 Americans for the Arts Johnson Fellowship for Artists Transforming Communities. Tiokasin is a professor at the Union Theological Seminary and the New School University – Parsons School of Design in New York City and is tri-authoring a book, *Earth Mind*.

Xiye Bastida

Xiye is a young Mexican climate activist, a Mother Earth defender, mobilizer, speaker, author and thought leader hailing from the Otomi-Toltec Indigenous community in Central Mexico. In 2020 she co-founded the Re-Earth Initiative and in 2021 she addressed world leaders at the Biden Climate Summit and at the annual UN Climate Conference. She also serves as a Fossil Fuel Non-Proliferation Treaty Champion and a Climate Governance Commissioner. Xiye was recognized by the United Nations with the UN Spirit Award. In 2023, she was named ELLE Woman of the Year and TIME100 Next 2023. She is an honour's student at the University of Pennsylvania.

https://www.xiyebeara.com/

Index

acceptance, 142
of death, 170–1
accountability, 42–4
Akkermansia muciniphila, 166–7
alliance, 46–7
antidepressants, statistics, 1–2
anxiety, 70
during the Covid pandemic, 54–5
facing up to, 116–18
statistics, 2
attention span, 49–51, 57
balance in nature, 110–14
Bifidobacterium, 165–6
biocultural heritage, 108
biotin, 178
boundaries, 31
brain
development, 27–9
neuroplasticity, 6
breathing, 123
Buddhism, xiii, xiii–xiv
interconnectedness, 38
meditation, 133
B-vitamins, 155–6, 176–8
calcium, 179
caregivers
anxiety, 54–5
'good enough', 35
relationship with school staff, 71
as role models, 32, 45–6, 58, 173
support from, 6–8
character education, 71–3
childhood cancer, 168–9
Children's Fire, The, 13–23
chromium, 180
cold water therapy, 124
collectivity, 105–8
communication, 32–5
compassion, 143
connectedness, 32–5

with water, xv, 97–104, 120–4
in Xhosa culture, 36–47
consciousness, awareness of, 143–4
copper in diet, 153–4, 180
Covid pandemic, 1, 52–5
death, acceptance of, 170–1
depression, statistics, 2
developmental stages, 26–7
diet, 147
common mistakes, 149–51
deficiencies, 152–62, 176–84
gut microbiome, 162–7
gut–brain axis, 148–9
and puberty, 151–2
digital technology
in the Covid pandemic, 52–3
as a distraction, 49–51, 57–8
in education, 52–4
healthy approach to use, 56–9
education, 131
character education, 71–3
during the Covid pandemic, 52–3
humanizing the classroom, 61–78
relationship between parents and
staff, 71
relationship between students and
teachers, 76–7
technology in, 52–4
emotional regulation, 31–2
essential fatty acids, 158–9, 181
focus, 49–51, 57
folic acid, 179
footwear industry, 79–85
gifts, 19–21
'golden age' fallacy, 55–6
gun violence, 3, 63
gut–brain axis, 148–9
gut health, 152–3, 162–7
happiness, 22
Hong Kong, 98
Hopi Elders' Prophecy, 174

humanity, 90–5, 127–8
  collectivity, 105–8
  as identity, 97
  purpose, 10–13, 16–23
identity
  knowing oneself, 93–4, 132
  with the world, 97
India, 133–4
Indigenous cultures, 126–30
inflammatory bowel disease (IBD), 163–4
interconnectedness, 36–47, 91
  with water, xv, 97–104
intergenerational alliance, 46–7
intergenerational trauma, 42
iodine, 181
iron in diet, 153, 155, 181
Jubilee Centre, 72
kindness, 77
kinship, 41–2
knowing oneself, 93–4, 132
L. reuteri, 163–5
Lactobacillus, 165–6
language, and understanding, 128–9
limbic system, 28
listening effectively, 32–5, 118
loneliness, 5, 89
love, 87
  deep and profound, 16–19
magnesium, 156–7, 182
manganese, 182
mantras, xvii
Māori culture, 37–8
meditation, xv, 133–9
  practices, 139–46
mental health, 132–3
  breakdown, 115–18
  causes of problems, 3–5
  gut–brain axis, 148–9
  statistics, 1–2
mindfulness, 117
molybdenum, 183
morals, 44–6
Mother Earth, 105–14
nature, being in, 145–6

nutrition, 147
  common mistakes, 149–51
  deficiencies, 152–62, 176–84
  gut–brain axis, 148–9
  gut microbiome, 162–7
  and puberty, 151–2
Oceanic Global, 96–7, 99–104
omega-3 fatty acids, 160–1
omega-6 fatty acids, 159
omega-9 fatty acids, 159
online safety, 59
parents
  anxiety, 54–5
  'good enough', 35
  relationship with school staff, 71
  as role models, 32, 45–6, 58, 173
  support from, 6–8
phosphorus, 183
potassium, 183
power, 15
prayer, 145
protein in diet, 161–2
puberty, 26–7
  and nutrition, 151–2
purpose of life, 10–13, 16–23
relativity, 128–9
responsibilities, 21–3
risk management, 29–31
school shootings, 3, 63
selenium, 183
self-harming, 4
smartphones, 3–4
social media, 3–5, 51
  regulating use, 56, 57–9
sound baths, 123–4
spirituality, xii, 133–8, 145–6
suicidality, statistics, 2
sulphur, 183
support, parental, 6–8
sustainability, 15, 17–18, 81–2
talking, 32–5
technology
  in the Covid pandemic, 52–3
  as a distraction, 49–51, 57–8

in education, 52–4
healthy approach to use, 56–9
Ubuntu, 39–41
ulcerative colitis (UC), 163–4
values, 44–6
vitamin A, 176
vitamin B, 155–6, 176–8
vitamin C, 179
vitamin D, 158, 180

vitamin E, 180
vitamin K, 181
'Vivo Way', 82–5, 108–9
water, human connection with, xv, 97–104, 120–4
workplace, humanizing, 82–5
Xhosa culture, 36–47
zinc in diet, 152–3, 154, 184

Notes

Join the Sheldon Press community today, sign up for our newsletter!

- Select a **FREE eBook** or extract to read upon joining

- Keep up with our latest publishing and exciting author news

- Be the first to hear about book prize draws, free extracts, and upcoming author events

Simply scan the QR code below or head to www.sheldonpress.co.uk/newsletter to sign up.